BUILDING
REAL ESTATE
WEALTH
in a CHANGING
MARKET

BUILDING
REAL ESTATE
WEALTH
in a CHANGING
MARKET

Reap Large Profits
from Bargain Purchases
in Any Economy

JOHN W. SCHAUB

McGraw-Hill

New York   Chicago   San Francisco   Lisbon
London   Madrid   Mexico City   Milan   New Delhi
San Juan   Seoul   Singapore   Sydney   Toronto

OCT 13 2007

The *McGraw·Hill* Companies

1 2 3 4 5 6 7 8 9 0   DOC/DOC   0 9 8 7

ISBN-13: 978-0-07-149412-0
ISBN-10: 0-07-149412-X

This publication is designed to provide accurate and authoritative information in regard to the subject matter covered. It is sold with the understanding that the publisher is not engaged in rendering legal, accounting, or other professional service. If legal advice or other expert assistance is required, the services of a competent professional person should be sought.
—From a Declaration of Principles Jointly Adopted by a
Committee of the American Bar Association and a
Committee of Publishers and Associations

McGraw-Hill books are available at special discounts to use as premiums and sales promotions, or for use in corporate training programs. For more information, please write to the Director of Special Sales, Professional Publishing, McGraw-Hill, Two Penn Plaza, New York, NY 10121-2298. Or contact your local bookstore.

This book is printed on acid-free paper.

Contents

Contents

Introduction

For 35 years I have adapted my investment strategy to change. Recessions, tax law changes, and fluctuating interest rates have all taken their best swing at the housing market. Through it all and in spite of periodic predictions of a housing collapse, house prices and rents have continued their steady climb.

Today the stage is set for a wave of distress selling and a new era of buying opportunities. Lenders have long forgotten the collapse of the real estate market in the 1980s. New young lenders are making many high-risk loans. Some of today's borrowers will become tomorrow's distressed sellers. The next few years will bring the opportunity of a lifetime to buy quality properties at bargain prices.

The future is bright for housing. Demand continues to increase. Baby boomers have charged into the market buying second and third homes. Now as the large wave of boomer kids enters the housing market, they are buying earlier, while in their early twenties. They are not waiting for the motivation of marriage or family that drove their parents to buy a house.

I just sold a house to a single man in his early twenties who plans on living in it with a roommate for a couple of years. He plans to buy another house and then another, based on the strategy I have followed and recommend.

Investing in houses is a time-tested way to accumulate significant wealth in a relatively short period of time. Some investors who have followed my advice have now surpassed $10 million in net worth. To do this you need knowledge and dedication, but not a lot of up-front capital or formal education.

The information in this book builds on my first book, *Building Wealth One House at a Time*, and, of course, I recommend that you read it. Learn to find opportunities where the reward is far greater than the risk, and then get in the game.

BUILDING
REAL ESTATE
WEALTH
in a CHANGING
MARKET

1

Embrace Change–It Will Never Stop

How do you like change? Change is not all that popular. It ruins well-made plans. Most of us would choose a totally predictable future for our investments if we could. Unfortunately, our investments are subject to the whims of the markets and the economy, and therefore are not predictable.

Successful investors not only adapt to change; they exploit it. While the majority of people sit on the sidelines wringing their hands, successful investors are looking for and buying opportunities created by the change.

When real estate markets change, denial is a popular first reaction. This is followed closely by the notion, "If we just keep doing the same thing, maybe it will work out."

Unlike the conventional wisdom in many sports, a good defense is not the best strategy in a changing real estate market. You need to invest safely, but when there is opportunity, you need a good offensive strategy.

Building Real Estate Wealth in a Changing Market

If you are to embrace change, you must look forward to it, reach out for it, anticipate it, and then you will be prepared for it. It will be good for you! If you react defensively, you will neither embrace change nor benefit from it.

Investing is by definition a conservative game. If you are taking wild chances with your money, you are not investing; you are speculating. In order to accumulate millions of dollars in assets and net worth, you must be an investor. A speculator may buy and sell millions of dollars' worth of property, but, in the end, all there will be to show for it is big stories. An investor may have fewer good stories but will have a lot more money.

You should not look for thrills from your investments; you want safety and growth. Get your thrills by spending some of your money skiing the black slopes in Aspen or scuba diving with the sharks. Wild swings in your net worth will get your heart pumping, but there are far less expensive ways to get excitement in your life.

You need an investment strategy that allows you to survive changes in the market without taking big losses. In fact, plan never to lose. If you lose 50% of your net worth, you now have to make a 100% after-tax profit to get back to even. Large losses set you back years and they can break your will to invest. It is critical that you have a plan to take advantage of changing markets without risking what you have accumulated.

If you are just getting started, then you probably have only a modest amount of money to lose. Believe it or not, you are in a better position to make your first million than the investor who just received a windfall and is afraid to lose it.

When you are broke, all that you have is your reputation. Of course, in the long run it is more important to guard your reputation than to protect your money. Your reputation with lenders is called your credit rating. Although you can invest without ever borrowing from banks, a good credit reputation will allow you to borrow at cheaper rates and to make better deals with a lender.

Predicting Change

Changes in the real estate market are not totally predictable, but it is a sure bet that we will continue to have both buyer's and seller's markets. They follow each other as naturally as a high tide follows a low tide. These changes are the natural effect of a market seeking balance when it is overbought or oversold.

Fortune-tellers like to predict the length of these cycles. What they may not recognize is that real estate markets are different throughout the country. On any day, one market may have 20%-a-year appreciation, another market chugs along at 4% or 5% appreciation, and another can be stagnant or declining. Money tends to flee the slower markets and fuel the hotter markets. Although I strongly advise you to invest in real estate where you live, if your town has no potential for growth, consider a move to a better market before you buy.

Although you cannot accurately predict changes, you can anticipate corrections in the market and prepare to take advantage of them. If your market has been a seller's market for several years with higher-than-average rates of appreciation, you should have the thought that we may be nearing the end of this run-up in prices and get yourself prepared for a slowdown or even a downturn in the market. This does not mean that you get out of the market; it may mean that you sell a few properties and pay off some high-risk debt, or build up your cash reserves.

This book will focus on residential real estate, although the principles and strategies covered are equally applicable to other types of real estate. It will discuss factors beyond your control that impact the market, including interest rates and the availability of credit, the tax laws, and the strength of the economy.

The real estate market is constantly changing and it always will. Embrace change and you will be prepared for it and profit from it. Those who ignore change often become its victims.

2

Causes of Change–
What Was Different
This Time?

When business is booming, everyone is working and interest rates are cheap; the housing market predictably expands.

A booming market attracts builders and speculators. Eventually, they will create too much inventory and the supply of houses will exceed the number of buyers. The prices will stop rising. And if the prices have risen well beyond the actual value of the property, they will drop or at least stop increasing until the existing inventory is sold.

In our most recent market, builders and speculators were asking for profits far in excess of a normal gain in a more balanced market. For example, a speculator or builder might buy a lot for $100,000, build a house for $200,000 and then try to sell it for $500,000. If he could buy, build, and sell in a year, he would make a before-tax profit of about $200,000 on his $300,000 investment. This is a far greater than normal profit, so when the market returns to normal, the speculator may make $50,000 to $100,000 on the same transaction. Of course, that is a gross profit and does not account for the cost of borrowing the money or paying the expenses during the building period. This is by no means a guaranteed profit. If hundreds of houses flood the market at the same time, the price may have to be reduced to give a buyer a bargain, reducing or eliminating the profit.

Whenever the market overheats and provides excessive profits for builders, developers, and speculators, it attracts more and more players until they create an oversupply. Then the profits return to more normal levels. Although there is no set profit margin you can depend on when buying and selling a house, you should set a minimum profit if you are going to play in this market. There is risk and you need to be compensated, not only for the use of your capital, but also for the risk you are taking to buy and sell short-term. A long-term investor may be happy to buy a property at 10% below the market when financing can be obtained that will allow an immediate return on the investment. A speculator better have a higher goal, because, as in the game of musical chairs, when the music stops, the speculator probably will get stuck with the last one that he or she bought and give back some of the profit.

Some writers have termed the end of the run-up in house prices "a bubble," implying that if the bubble bursts, then prices will drop dramatically. Although prices can drop dramatically in the stock market, and land prices and prices on commercial properties are subject to large swings, residential prices of moderately priced houses, where "everyman" lives, are historically more stable.

There are a number of reasons that house prices are more stable than prices of raw land or office buildings or commercial buildings. First, people live in houses and nobody likes to move. People will struggle to keep their home. Renters will scrimp on other items in their budget to stay in a good house in a good neighborhood. This resistance to packing up and moving helps stabilize the market. On the other hand, if a business goes broke, it has to move. Statistically, according to the National Federation of Independent Business Educational Foundation, small businesses make high-risk tenants, with only 39% of them ever turning a profit.

In any market, there are potential buyers. Most buyers of median-priced houses make their buying decision based on the amount of the down payment and the monthly payment. The total price of the house is secondary to these two very real numbers; reality strikes when someone has to write a check at closing and have funds in the bank every month for the mortgage payment. See Figure 2–1 for an illustration of the relationship between median house prices and fed funds rates for the years 1967–2007.

Therefore, when credit is loose and interest is cheap, house prices tend to jump because many more people can afford to buy and this creates competition for the existing supply of houses. As

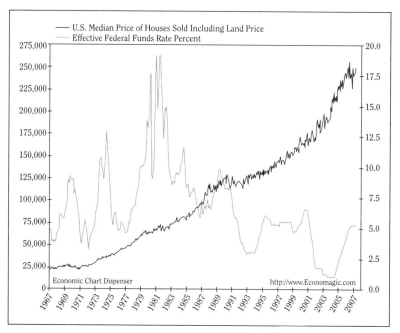

Figure 2–1   Median House Prices and the Federal Funds Rate (1967–2007)

buyers compete, they drive prices higher. Those higher prices now attract more builders, and more inventory is created. Speculators jump into the market, buying from builders and other sellers, and reselling for quick profits.

Many of these buyers (the end users) are coming from the rental market. When they can buy a house with monthly payments equal to their rent or a reasonable amount more, they become buyers. Nearly everyone would rather own than rent, and will pay more than their current rent as a house payment where they are building equity and perhaps picking up some tax deductions.

As the renters compete to buy, the demand for rentals decreases. Many landlords take advantage of the rising market to sell at a profit. This reduces the amount of inventory available for rentals. Eventually, rents will increase as the demand for rentals increases and the supply remains low.

At some point in the cycle, the cost of buying in terms of the monthly payment is so much greater than the cost of renting, that some potential buyers decide to rent instead. Table 2–1 displays some real numbers from my market (Sarasota, Florida) over the last 10 years.

As the interest rates dropped, prices started up as the monthly payment became more attractive compared with the rent. When tenants could afford to buy a house for less than the cost to rent, renters became buyers. As prices increased rapidly, although interest rates remained low, the monthly loan payment eventually became higher than the rents.

Some creative lenders made loans with less-than-interest-only payments. This enables buyers to borrow more money than they could normally qualify for. Unfortunately for those borrowers, many such loans have both variable interest rates and short terms. As the rates increase and the loans come due, many of the borrowers will not be able to qualify for a new loan, putting their homes and credit in jeopardy.

Table 2-1 Average House Prices and Payments in Sarasota, Florida (1997–2006)

Year	House Price	Rent	Interest Rate (30-year fixed rate as of June)	Monthly Payment 30-Year Loan* (95% Loan)
1997	$90,000	$720	8.5%	$657
1998	$95,000	$760	7.9%	$655
1999	$100,000	$800	7.1%	$638
2000	$105,000	$850	7.7%	$711
2001	$110,000	$900	8.4%	$796
2002	$118,000	$950	7.3%	$768
2003	$138,000	$975	6.7%	$845
2004	$180,000	$975	6.4%	$1,069
2005	$240,000	$1,000	5.8%	$1,337
2006	$250,000	$1,100	6.8%	$1,548
2007	$250,000	$1,200	6.9%	$1,564

* These are principal and interest payments only. Taxes and insurance would add a significant amount to the mortgage payment.

As sellers sold the less expensive houses, they began to buy more expensive houses and this wave of buying trickled up the market.

Notice that rents creep up at about 5% a year in most years, leveling off when many renters become buyers and leaving landlords competing to fill vacancies. When house prices stop going up, renters will again begin to compete for rentals, pushing rents up at a higher-than-average rate.

Boomers Are Demanding Bigger Houses

One factor that is pushing up the average and median price of a house sold is that builders are building bigger and more elaborate houses than they did 20 years ago. In the 1950s, '60s, and '70s, millions of basic three-bedroom, one- and two-bath homes, in the

1,200- to 1,400-square-foot range were built. This created an inventory of relatively affordable houses.

Today, few builders build a basic house or a small house. Condos have replaced the smaller homes as the "starter houses" of this century. Many older apartments houses have been converted to condominiums. These are smaller units and they are inexpensive because many of them can be built on the amount of land it would take to construct one house.

The primary factor driving builders to build bigger and more expensive houses is the cost of land. In most growing areas, governments have responded to the cries of existing homeowners asking for slow growth, less traffic, and for growth to pay its own way. This has driven land prices higher, and builders will continue to build more expensive homes as long as there is a market for them.

There are still millions of moderately sized houses built in the 1960s through the early 1980s that make both excellent investments and great homes in which to live. In a changing market these houses will become more attractive to buyers because they are more affordable and less expensive to maintain.

It's the Land That Appreciates

A house investor needs to keep in mind that the appreciation in any house is caused by the rising value of the land, not the house. Houses actually wear out, become obsolete, and often become less desirable. Older houses are often torn down and replaced by newer, more expensive houses as the value of the lot far exceeds the value of the house.

Beware of buying a large, expensive-to-maintain home as an investment. The more moderate home on a great lot will appreciate more and yield higher net income than the larger house.

The ratio of house value to lot value will impact the appreciation of a property. As it is the lot that is appreciating, a $100,000 house on a $200,000 lot will be a better long-term investment than a $200,000 house on a $100,000 lot.

3

Predicting Change in Your Market

While you cannot predict the future, you can anticipate change by staying attuned to a number of factors in your market.

Take both a macro and micro view of your market. In the macro, or larger, view, study your demographics. Is your town growing? Will it continue to be a desirable place to live, attracting many new buyers? Which part of town is likely to see the greatest appreciation in the next decade or two?

If the prospects for your town are good, a short-term downturn in the market should not discourage you from buying. In fact, it is a real buying opportunity and you can make big up-front profits buying well below the market in a buyer's market.

If your town is overly dependent on one industry or employer, the long-term prospects for that industry or company are a key part of your analysis. Towns tend to adjust over time to the loss of a major employer, but it can take a long time. There was a time when the hiring policy of Boeing Aircraft had a major influence on the Seattle housing market. Today, Boeing is still a factor, but thousands of new jobs have given Seattle the diversity necessary to absorb any layoffs from Boeing. There are hundreds of examples of this type of successful transition in cities like Boston, Charlotte, and San Diego, but it takes time for new jobs to replace lost ones.

On the micro, or smaller view, you need to recognize what part of the cycle you are in and plan your buying strategy so that you both survive and prosper in a changing market. When house prices peak, you want to sell if you need to, and when they bottom out, you will want to buy all the bargains that you can afford.

If you don't want to try to predict how your market will change, you can use the simple plan of just buying one house a year until you have enough. Good deals are available in every market, and as you continue to buy, you will hone your skills and make better and better deals. Of course if you buy more when sellers are giving away property and sell when buyers are standing in line to pay too much, you can make your fortune faster and it will be bigger.

Rents and House Prices

When the amount of rent landlords can charge becomes high in relation to the price, tenants will aggressively begin to look to buy.

Landlords raise rents as often as they can because they have ever-increasing expenses. However, they can only raise rents when the vacancy rate is relatively low and tenants are competing for a limited supply of houses.

You can track the number of houses available by following the Sunday classified section of your local paper. Count the number of columns (or number of ads if it is small) of houses for rent each Sunday. Chart it, and you will get a feel for the number of empty houses in your town. Obviously not every empty house is advertised, but the number of ads will give you an indication of the number of vacancies. As the Internet becomes a bigger factor in advertising property, you will be able to use the information on it to track the availability and prices of rentals.

The Credit Market

Many tenants would rather buy than rent, but they cannot save up the down payment or qualify for a loan because of their credit. In some markets, lenders relax their lending standards, allowing buyers to borrow 100% of the purchase price with payments of less-than-interest-only. When this happens, many people who could not ordinarily qualify to buy a house win the lottery and get a loan. Unfortunately, many of those loans will later fall into default when interest rates rise, foreclosures increase, and lenders once again tighten their lending standards. This is a natural cycle, fueled in part by the bad memories (and turnover) of the lenders. Lenders make money when they originate loans. They charge up-front fees and then charge again when collecting the loan payments (servicing fees). They then sell these loans to another lender or to institutional buyers like Fannie Mae or Freddie Mac, who raise money in the securities markets by selling bonds. When these loans are sold, the buyer may reserve the right to get money back if the loan goes into default. This leaves the originator of the loan with some residual liability. When a foreclosure occurs, the original lender has to buy back the loan and then deal with the foreclosure.

The Number of Foreclosures

As foreclosures are advertised in a local newspaper, you can track their number. When you see a sharp rise in the number of foreclosures, you can anticipate a tightening credit market. Lenders who are foreclosing on loans will become more careful about making loans. This will make it increasingly difficult for new buyers to qualify, and will have a cooling effect on the housing market.

The Sales Price That Foreclosures Bring at the Sale

Lenders track not only the number of foreclosure sales, but how much the properties are selling for at these auctions. When there are many bidders at a foreclosure auction, then the bidders will compete for the properties and bid up the price. When this happens, often the lenders will recover all or most of their investment in the loan.

However, as a market becomes more of a buyer's market and fewer buyers are willing to bid on foreclosure properties, their bids will be much lower. Then lenders will have to choose between taking a loss and letting the property sell for less than their loan balance, or taking title to the property and trying to sell it for more than the bid.

As more properties sell for less than the loan balances, smart lenders choose to help their existing borrowers to survive rather than be so quick to foreclose.

Attend your local foreclosure auctions occasionally, not to bid on property, but to count the number of bidders and to compare the bids with the loan balances. You may have to attend these auctions a few times to figure out the system, but ask questions of the trustee or clerk conducting the auction. They are typically willing to answer your questions or will tell you how to get them answered.

Beware of high-priced foreclosure seminars that promise easy profits with minimum risk. Foreclosure buying is the riskiest way to buy property. The terms are all cash, and there are no warranties or guarantees on anything. You get what you get. The house could be stripped of everything valuable and trashed before you can get possession. One successful buyer came to me after a local foreclosure auction after he had learned that the property he bought was subject to a $120,000 lien that was not wiped out by the sale. He had paid about twice what the property was worth, and it was too late to be seeking professional advice. Never bid on a foreclosure property without competent legal counsel on your team. After the sale, you have no recourse against anyone. That's why it is so risky.

The Average Time to Sell a Listing–The Number of Active Listings and the Number of Listings Sold

Although not every property for sale is listed with a real estate agent, a representative number are, so that by tracking the sales of local agents, you can get a good feel for how long it will take to sell a property. Realtors are real estate agents who share their listings through Multiple Listing Services (MLS), and who belong to the local Realtor Association.

When an agent with access to MLS gets a live buyer, the agent is not limited to her listings, although she will make more money if she sells her listing. Chances are the agent will try hard to do just that.

Every listing and every sale are tracked, and facts like the average number of days on the market, the average sales prices as a percentage of the listing price, and the number of listings that are sold and never sold are published.

Even if you are not an agent, you can access this information by requesting it from an agent with whom you work. By comparing this data on a quarterly basis, you can see trends in the market.

It is good to compare one quarter's data with that of the same quarter the previous year, not just with that of the immediately previous quarter. Spring and summer typically produce more sales than fall and winter, so if you compare the spring quarter to the winter quarter, you might conclude that the market is getting better, when it is actually only the weather that is improving.

The Number of New Building Permits

Your local building department tracks the number of new building permits and also permits for new subdivisions. The number of new permits will peak at the end of a bull market in house prices. While it's difficult to determine before it happens, a significant drop in the number of new permits will confirm for you that the market has switched from a seller's to a buyer's market.

The Ratio between the Cost of a New House and Its Sale Price

As a market heats up, sellers and builders are able to charge a premium when they sell a house. The amount of this premium depends on the strength of the market. The stronger the market, the higher the premium.

For example, if you can buy a lot for $100,000, and build a house for $200,000, it might sell in a normal market for some small premium over the total cost of $300,000, because a buyer will pay more for instant gratification. In a normal market, a builder might command a premium of $25,000 or even $50,000. In a hot market, the same house may bring a $100,000 or even a $200,000 premium. This is an artificial boost in value, and this premium quickly disappears when the market reverses.

In a down market, it does not cost much less to build a house, or to buy land and develop a lot. The water and sewer lines, the sidewalks and streets are still just as expensive to install. What might change is the product that the builders deliver. They may build a smaller house with fewer luxury items in order to deliver a house at a significantly lower price. This can cause the average price of a new house sold to drop dramatically from one year to the next as the market changes.

Don't Be Fooled by the Averages

Averages can be very deceiving if you do not compare apples with apples. When the number of house sales drops, often the more expensive houses will stop selling first. There are some exceptions to this rule for the very high priced houses—because buyers of $5 million and $10 million houses are less sensitive to market changes than buyers of $300,000 houses.

It is obvious that when the higher-priced houses stop selling, the average price of a house will drop. For example, let's assume there were four sales of houses in month one in your town, as listed in Table 3–1.

Table 3–1   Houses Sold in a Town over Two-Month Period

	Month One	Month Two
House 1	$100,000	$100,000
House 2	$200,000	$200,000
House 3	$200,000	$200,000
House 4	$500,000	
Total	$1,000,000	$500,000

That month the average price of a house sold was $250,000 (the total sales of $1,000,000 divided by the four sales). If the following month only three houses sell, for a total of $500,000, the average sale price that month would be $166,666 ($500,000 divided by 3). Did any of the houses actually go down in value?

Only a few financial reporters are savvy enough to actually compare the real price of a house sold with what it sold for previously to determine a trend.

The national publications often address the real estate market as if it was a national market. Nothing could be farther from reality. Every state, every county within that state, and neighborhoods within those counties are unique. Houses can be going up in value in one neighborhood in your town and down in another.

On-the-Street Surveys

Drive through neighborhoods in your town and notice how many houses are for sale and for rent. Make this effort often and you will notice how your neighborhoods are doing. Often the newspaper will publish a provocative story, touting either a hot market or, conversely, a crashing market. They rarely run a story saying everything is going just right. Those who rely on the paper for information might be influenced by these stories, but if you are in touch with your markets and know what the inventory is doing where you buy, your decisions will be based on facts not hype.

I suggest that you track specific houses in the neighborhoods where you want to own property. When a house sells, find out the sales price and then compare it with the price it sold for the last time. This information is typically available to you from your county tax assessor; these records are online in many counties. There are Web sites, like www.zillow.com, that also provide values and can give you some round-figure information, but I would not rely on such sites without confirming the prices with the public records.

Public Records Can Contain Mistakes

Note that even the public records may not be entirely accurate. The county receives its information from sellers and closing agents. Occasionally mistakes are made, and at times sellers overstate the price to prop up values in a neighborhood. Especially in a falling market, builders and other sellers want higher sales prices reported, so that appraisers will continue to appraise at high prices.

By paying attention to your market, you will know when prices are at levels that are too high or too low. You will know when rents are a bargain and have upside potential, as well as when they are high relative to the values of the houses. Although no one can accurately predict the day or month that a market will turn around, you can recognize the factors that lead to these turns and be prepared for them.

4

How Neighborhoods Change and How to Profit from the Change

Whenever someone moves in or out of a neighborhood, it changes. When a renter displaces an owner-occupant, the change is rarely for the better.

Conversely, when an owner-occupant replaces a renter when a landlord sells to a tenant, good results can occur. The excited new owners typically fix up or remodel their new home. They take pride in ownership and keep their yard well trimmed. Even their cars look better, and most don't park in the middle of the yard or drop a transmission in the driveway.

Neighbors change, and if you study the change in the neighborhood where you want to buy you will spot the trends.

From New to Used in 60 Seconds

When a neighborhood is brand-new, every house looks nearly perfect from the outside: the roofs are new, the paint is fresh, the yards uncluttered.

Then people move in and it goes downhill from there. Kids and pets dig holes in the lawns, and scatter toys and other surprises. One neighbor will have a green thumb and a lawn as fit as a putting green. But the couch potato next door will watch TV while the weeds return his yard to its natural, unmanicured state.

As the roofs wear out and the houses need work, some owners sell and move on. Landlords of other properties will purchase some of these houses. A few will fix them up so that they look like new again, while the others will rent them to tenants who don't mind living in a house that needs painting and a new roof. These less picky tenants will move in with their own special additions, like the car with no fender and a collection of dogs.

Looking for Opportunity

Now that you understand neighborhood cycles, you can begin to look for them in your target neighborhoods. When is the best time to buy in a neighborhood? Certainly not when it is brand-new, unless you get a great bargain.

The best time to buy is when you can see clearly that renters are being replaced by owners, as a result of landlord sales.

Creating Opportunity

You can help this process along by contacting landlords who own neglected properties in otherwise good neighborhoods, and buying from them. As a smart landlord, you can fix up the houses and then rent them to tenants who will be an asset to the neighborhood and who will value the property and take care of it.

Buy the weakest house on a street from a worn-out landlord, and then make it look as good as the other houses. You will improve the property value of every house on the street, and your house will jump in value.

When you buy a run-down house, make sure you get it at a "run-down" price. You have an advantage over many buyers as you can agree to buy the property in "as is" condition, after carefully inspecting the house for defects. Make it easy for a landlord to sell and you are more likely to make a good deal.

Some landlords will finance the purchase when they sell to you. They have an aversion to both paying taxes and earning the low interest that a bank would pay them. If they sell to you and carry the financing, they can pay taxes as they receive their profits.

Plus, they can keep their full equity earning interest, not just the after-tax equity that they would have if they sold for cash and paid taxes. Also, they can charge you more interest than the bank will pay them. Today they might get 2% to 5% from a bank, while you can afford to pay 5.5% or 6%. It's a great deal for both of you.

A landlord is used to taking risks. They probably rent this house for $1,400 to $1,600 a month and let a perfect stranger move in with only one month's rent and a deposit up front. You can offer them several times that amount of money as a down payment and still have the high leverage, which will give you a fantastic return.

Case Study: A House Purchased from a Landlord

House value:	$250,000–$275,000
Your purchase price:	$225,000 (as is)
Your down payment:	$10,000
Your monthly payments on $215,000	
at 5.5% for 30 years:	$1,120.76

If a landlord sells to you and finances $215,000 of the purchase price at 5.5% interest, it would yield a monthly income of $1,120.76.

If instead the landlord sells for cash, pays taxes, and invests the money in a bank, how much money would that yield each month?

Example of a landlord's after-tax income (for a sale of $225,000):

Sale price:	$225,000
Taxes:	$25,000
Value after taxes:	$200,000
Yearly income (@ 5%):	$10,000
Monthly income:	$833.33

Compare this with $1,120 a month less the tax due only on the share of the landlord's profit received that month ($150,000/360 = $416 × 15% = $62.40 in tax due on the profit). The interest earned in the bank or on the note would be taxable.

Solving Neighborhood Problems for Profit

Sometimes you don't have to buy a house to improve the property values in a neighborhood. John Adams, a friend who lives in Atlanta and teaches house investing, tells this story about a neighbor who was creating a problem. John owned a house on a first-rate street near the Emory University campus. Unfortunately his next-door neighbor was a collector. She collected older cars, all in need of repair. This was an irritation to John, who kept his property in good condition and wanted to attract great tenants.

One day he saw the neighbor in the yard and approached her about all the old cars. He learned that the cars had belonged to her husband who had passed away some years before, and although she would love to get rid of them, she did not know how to do it.

John agreed to get the job done for her and she was delighted. He added thousands of dollars to the value of his property and that of the other houses on that street by doing a good deed.

Profit from Neighborhood Change

If you see neighbors in distress, offer to help. By doing the neighbors a favor, for instance, helping them find a good painter or landscaper or roofer, you might make a friend and improve the street where you own property.

Occasionally, you might even buy a house! (Don't forget to ask if they want to sell.)

5

Setting Your Strategy for Buying in a Changing Market

Even when the market is changing, your business and financial goals should not change dramatically. Because it is easier to buy property does not mean that you should buy many more properties than you planned. You should just buy enough property to get you to your goal.

If you don't have a plan, now is the time to consider how many properties you want to buy, what type of property you want to buy, and how you want to buy it.

How Many?

My plan is to buy as few properties as possible to meet my financial goals. Every property that you buy has both potential profit and potential problems. Every property that you buy will take some of your time, and your time is the one thing that money cannot replace. When people brag about buying 100 houses a year, you wonder why anyone would want to do all that work and take that amount of risk.

In 35 years of full-time investing, I have acquired fewer than 200 properties. That's an average of about 5 a year, and I work at it full-time. Given another chance, I would buy fewer properties. The apartments, the duplexes, the motels, and commercial buildings all required far too much time for the profits they produced. Houses that attracted long-term, low-maintenance tenants were by far my best investments.

Knowing that in a buyer's market it will be easier to buy than to sell, you want to buy only one house at a time, unless you are both experienced and well funded. Even then, you can accumulate more real estate than you will ever need, by just buying one at a time.

Specialize

Investment advisors will tell you to diversify your investments. That is not bad advice if you are buying stocks and bonds. Any company can go belly-up, so you want to spread your risk.

When buying property, the advantages of specialization out-weigh the risk involved. If you are going to invest in houses, you can diversify your risk by buying houses on different streets and in different neighborhoods. If one neighborhood or street does not appreciate, others will.

The advantage of specialization is that you will learn values and rents in a certain type of property in certain neighborhoods. You must know the value of a property, what it will rent for, and the market for that particular property before you make an offer. Knowing what something is worth allows you to make offers at below-market prices. Knowing what monthly rent a good tenant will pay allows you to borrow money on terms that the property will repay.

As I noted above, early in my career I purchased many different types of property. Unfortunately, I was not an expert on the market for any of those properties, so I did not make great deals when I bought them. You cannot become an expert in every type of property, so pick one type and learn as much as you can about buying and managing it.

Another big benefit of specialization is that you can develop your management system to manage just one type of tenant. Each type of property—houses, apartments, commercial space, offices—has unique tenants. Each requires different leases, different strategies to attract tenants, and different levels of attention.

Once I owned a commercial building leased to a restaurant. If there was a problem, it had to be fixed within an hour; the restaurant would lose thousands of dollars in revenue for each hour it could not open for business. What would be an inconvenience to a residential tenant was an emergency to a commercial tenant that needed an immediate response.

By renting to just one type of tenant, you can have clear and standardized policies and paperwork. Single-family residential tenants are by far the easiest to manage once you understand how to manage.

Buy the Best Properties That You Can Afford

Better-located properties appreciate more and attract better tenants. Buyers often pay a premium for a good house on a good street. In down markets, some of the best properties in town may become available at bargain prices. You have to be a contrarian to buy when all others are selling, but that is when you will make your best buys. Identify the neighborhoods that have the most potential for appreciation in your town, and set a goal to buy there, if not today, one day.

When you start buying, the best property that you can afford to own may be an older house or a duplex or a small apartment building. You can squeeze more monthly cash flow out of these types of properties, but you will spend more time managing the tenants that these buildings attract. The tenants tend to move more, and rarely improve the property. When they leave, you will often have to invest both your time and money to get the unit in shape to rent again.

Because they require more time to manage, fewer buyers want to own them. Although you can make a good return while you own them, when you sell, you will have to make the next buyer a good deal to entice them to buy. Your gain or profit when you sell will be smaller than if you bought a better-located property that would be in higher demand.

Buying to Resell for Short-Term Cash Flow

The business of buying and selling houses requires a higher skill level than buying houses to hold long-term. When you buy to resell, you have to buy at a deeper discount, and you have to buy something that you can resell quickly. If you buy a house and cannot sell it quickly, your potential profit will soon disappear. If you are buying and reselling to other investors, your profits will be small, because they too will be looking to make a profit. The good part of reselling to another investor is that you can often do this in only a few days or weeks.

Before you buy a house to resell, check with a real estate agent to see which price ranges and which neighborhoods are selling the fastest. In a slow market, it will take months instead of weeks to sell a house, even at a low price. Know the average time on the market for the house that you plan to buy so that you can project your holding costs and have the money on hand to make the payments until it sells. If you are short on cash to cover the monthly payments, you may be tempted to accept an offer for thousands less than you could get if you could hold out one or two more months.

If you buy and then sell to a buyer who will live in the house, you are likely to make a larger profit, but you have to wait longer to collect it. Most homebuyers have to qualify for and close on a new loan in order to buy your house. This can take a month or longer, after you find the buyer. In a slow market, it can take many months to get an offer.

Working Less and Earning More after Taxes

Short-term profits from buying and selling a house are taxed at the higher ordinary income rate. Higher net profits can be created if you buy, hold, and rent the house for at least a year, and then sell to qualify for long-term capital gains.

Compare the two sales shown in Table 5–1.

If your goal was to produce $100,000 a year in annual income, you can do it by buying and selling six houses in 12 months, or you could generate the same $100,000 a year in after-tax income with only two purchases and sales a year if your plan is to hold the houses for two years before you sell.

Buying six houses at bargain prices, and then reselling and closing them in six months would take both a high level of skill

Table 5–1 Long- and Short-Term House Sales Compared

	Short-Term Resale House	Longer-Term Resale House
Market value	$300,000	$300,000
Purchase price	$250,000	$270,000
Holding period	3 months	2 years
Sale price (net)	$275,000 (wholesale)	$330,000 (retail)
Tax	$7,500 (30%)	$9,000 (15%)
Net profit	$17,500	$51,000

and a lot of work. In a slow market, buying may be easy, but selling and getting all six to close would be challenging.

You can see from this comparison, that a business plan that allowed you to hold houses for at least two years (assuming a 5%-a-year average increase in value) would produce significantly more profit than a plan of buying and immediately reselling. Notice that the buyer who bought and held two years actually paid more for the property (he did not have to buy as far below the market), but still made more profit because of the combination of some small increase in value combined with a lower tax rate.

You might be in a lower tax bracket if the only income you have is from buying and selling one or two houses a year. However, if you have other income, or buy and sell many houses a year, your tax rate could be 30% or higher, plus any local or state tax you may have to pay. The only real profit is an after-tax profit. Always consider what your net income will be when putting together your plan.

The one problem with buying and selling houses for cash flow is that you can't stop working or your cash flow stops. It's a job: a well-paying job that can be fun and exciting, but it's still a job. You can quit working when you transition from buying and selling to investing. You can use many of the same skills, especially those involving buying and negotiating, and actually make more money with less effort.

Buying Houses That Produce Long-Term Cash Flow

In my seminar, "Making It Big on Little Deals," I teach that you can make more money than you can ever spend, by investing safely in just one house at a time.

Conservative investors are the ones that pile up huge fortunes, and they do it by never taking big losses. If your losses are all "little deals," then you will never have to start over again, and you will never be out of the market. On the other hand, little deals grow up to be big deals when you hold them until they mature.

Setting Your Strategy for Buying in a Changing Market

Investing in moderately priced houses allows you to take high risk from a leverage standpoint. That is, you can borrow 100% (or close to it) of the purchase price with some comfort. You can use this amount of leverage in any market. If you buy a house with nothing down and it goes down in value, now the lender has a problem along with you. If the lender was the seller, you have an opportunity to approach him or her and renegotiate the price or terms.

If the lender was not the seller, you certainly have an obligation to repay any money you borrowed. However, the lender may be open to negotiating lower payments to encourage you to keep paying. When prices drop below loan balances and owners find themselves upside down (the loan balance is higher than the value of the property), many owners simply stop making payments and walk away from the property.

Compare that to the amount of leverage you can comfortably use buying stocks or other types of investments and you can see why more people make their first million in real estate than in the stock market.

The housing market is historically stable compared to other markets, so lenders are willing to lend a greater percentage of the purchase price.

Being able to use leverage to buy an investment with a long-term history of steady appreciation gives you the opportunity to turn a small amount of money into a large fortune in a fraction of a lifetime. That's good, because many people don't start investing until they are in their forties, fifties, or even their sixties.

The secret to not taking losses is to buy just one house at a time. One of my students attended the seminar several times, and then proudly called me to announce that he had just bought 13 houses at one time. Unfortunately, the next day he owned 13 empty houses and had to learn to manage in a hurry. The other unfortunate part was that the seller was a more experienced investor (the seller bought the houses one at a time), so my student paid more per house than he would have had he purchased one at a time.

Buying houses one at a time is safer in a changing market. If prices are dropping, then you want to buy cautiously, if at all, until you see some sign of a price reversal. It is nearly impossible to predict either the top or the bottom of a market.

After the market peaks, the press has a heyday printing stories about buyers who paid high prices and now are stuck with property worth less than they paid for it. The examples that they use often show how far a house has dropped from the peak of the market. If you are unfortunate enough to buy at the exact peak, you want to buy only one property.

If you did buy a property at or near the top of the market, you need to compare the cost of selling it today and taking a loss with the cost of holding it until you can reasonably expect the market to rebound.

All markets are different, but it will typically take several years for an overbuilt housing market to right itself. How long it will take depends on how overbuilt your market is and on the number of buyers moving to your town each year. It takes new population to reduce the inventory.

When making your projections, plan to hold the property for at least three years. If you plan on holding it until the property doubles in value, then use a 10-year term to be conservative. Rents will increase, and often increase at greater rates when the sales market is flat, as more people choose to rent than buy in a flat market. In *Building Wealth One House at a Time*, you will find a detailed plan for systematically accumulating houses. When you buy houses to hold long-term, the price that you pay today is not as important to you as the terms of the financing.

If your plan is to hold a house until it doubles in value, you need at least a 10-year loan, with the lowest payments that you can negotiate. The lower your payments, the more cash flow you will have for 10 years.

You cannot control the amount of income you will collect. You can learn to be an efficient manager and keep your houses full of good tenants, but you have no control over the amount of rent that you can charge. The market rent (the rent you can charge a tenant) will fluctuate with the demand for rentals and the supply of rentals that day.

In some markets, the demand is seasonal. In warmer states like Florida and Arizona, demand for rentals increases in the winter and rents typically rise.

Rents tend to mirror house prices over time, increasing on an average of about 5% a year in most markets. However, when prices are jumping, rents are often flat, as many renters become buyers. When the market changes and renters quit buying, then more renters are competing for a fixed supply of rental properties and rents tend to increase at a more rapid pace.

Selling Slowly for Maximum Profits

In the earlier comparison of buying and selling houses, two houses sold over two years produced more net income with less work than six houses sold the same year they were purchased. A long-term investor can be even more efficient, selling only when buyers are paying premium prices and buying when sellers are discounting prices.

If you hold a house 10 years before reselling, the profits from that one house may be large enough to support you for a year or longer. Look at the simplified plan in Table 5–2, where an investor buys one house a year and then begins selling one house a year when the first one doubles in value. The time that it will take for a house to increase in value to twice your purchase price will vary. As suggested in Table 5–2, if you become a skilled buyer and learn to buy 20%–30% below the market, then you have, in effect, bought two or three years' appreciation.

Table 5–2 Buying and Selling Houses for Profit over Time

	House Bought		Houses Sold in 10 Years*	
	Market Value	Purchase Price	Sales Price	Profit
Year 1	$250,000	$225,000	$500,000	$275,000
Year 2	$262,000	$230,000	$524,000	$294,000
Year 3	$275,000	$240,000	$550,000	$310,000

*Approximate time frame.

When you hold each house until it is worth at least twice the amount you paid to buy it, a sale 10 years after the purchase will produce hundreds of thousands of dollars in profits that will be taxed at low capital gains rates.

Of course you can sell a house after one year, five years, or hold it forever. The longer that you hold an income-producing, appreciating investment, the more money you will have in the future.

Seek Out Sellers with High Equities

An owner with a larger equity typically has a larger profit. Sellers with big profits are easier to buy from than a seller who is losing money. A seller with a significant profit will often lower the price thousands of dollars, if you just ask. They are comparing the sales price with the purchase price they paid for the house years ago.

Another advantage of buying from a seller who has a large equity is that they can afford to finance the sale for you if you buy their house. If you make them an offer giving them a down payment and a series of payments, rather than an all-cash offer, you may be able to pay them a higher price and still make a profit.

If you are buying the house to hold as an investment, then the terms of the financing are more important to you than the price. To make a significant profit on a house, you must hold it for enough time for it to double or more than double in value. The key to holding a house is having payments that you can afford during the holding period. If you can afford the payments, then you can hold the house indefinitely, until it hits your target profit.

A seller with a large profit and equity is your best prospect for carrying owner financing. Look for sellers in this situation and offer to buy their house, if they will finance your purchase on terms that make the house affordable for you.

Establish Your Minimum Profit Before You Make an Offer

Before you make an offer, set a profit goal for a house in that price range, based on the risk that you are taking. Use ranges when you value a house or make projections, because in the real world there is not one price that a house is worth or for which it will rent.

If you are buying a lower-priced house that you are confident you can immediately rent or resell for a small profit, then your risk is small and a $10,000 profit may compensate you adequately for your risk and time. As you buy more expensive properties that have higher carrying costs and will take longer to sell, your risk increases, and your minimum profit should increase.

If you are able and willing to take on the higher-risk properties, then you can make larger profits. If you are new to investing, keep your risk small until you have the confidence and cash in the bank to back you up when you take on larger risk. Table 5–3 is an example of prices and minimum profits an experienced investor would look for in a town where the median-priced house is worth $300,000.

Notice that Table 5–3 lists minimum profit "targets." A target is not hit every time. In addition, we occasionally get lucky and overshoot our targets. The purpose of setting this target is to give you a hard number to negotiate for so that you have a reasonable chance of making a profit. The more expensive properties are less

Table 5-3   Minimum Profit Targets When Selling Houses

House Price	Minimum Profit Target
$50,000–$100,000	$10,000
$100,000–$150,000	$20,000
$150,000–$200,000	$30,000
$200,000–$300,000	$40,000
$300,000–$400,000	$50,000
$400,000–$500,000	$100,000

liquid and will take longer to sell. You can probably buy and sell several $200,000 houses in the time it will take you to sell one $500,000 house. Because the less expensive houses sell faster, they are much safer to buy. However, as your buying skills improve, you might be able to buy a $500,000 house at $100,000 or even $200,000 below the market value. Your carrying costs will be higher, and you will have to be a patient seller, or you won't get to collect the full profit.

If you are buying a house that needs repairs, be sure to use today's value when calculating your minimum profit. You will hear people say that a house will be worth $400,000 *when it is fixed up*. That number bears no relation to what it is worth today. It may need $50,000 or $150,000 in work to be worth $400,000. Use today's values, not wishful thinking, to set your profit and then your offer.

Structuring Your Debt to Reduce Your Risk and Increase Your Profits

Not all loans are created equal. Some have higher risk than others. Your banker may understand what increases the risk on a loan, but few borrowers do.

You can reduce your risk if you know what increases it and negotiate with your lender to eliminate as many factors that increase your risk as possible. What's good for the lender is typically bad for the borrower, so it is a negotiation.

Before you borrow to buy a property, review the six factors discussed below and negotiate to reduce your risk. If the only way you can buy is with a high-risk loan, you may want to look for a safer opportunity, especially when the market is changing or uncertain.

1. Term of the Loan. A short-term loan, one that must be repaid in only a few years, is far riskier than a long-term loan. The longer-term loan gives you, the borrower, the right to keep the money for the term of the loan without paying any additional fees or requalifying. A short-term loan must be paid off and probably paid off with a new loan that you must both qualify for and then pay the costs of acquiring. When rates are low, always borrow for the longest term that you can negotiate. A 40-year loan is better than a 30-year loan because the payments will be a little lower. Lower payments make the loan safer. Some loans may have prepayment penalties, but they typically phase out in the first few years, so you have the option to pay off a loan and borrow at a cheaper rate if interest rates drop.

2. The Payment Schedule. Having a loan with a lower-than-normal payment for the first few years is a great idea, as long as you don't break rule number one, and you can afford the higher payments as they increase. Lower payments make the loan safer for you. Often a lender will charge a higher interest rate or some prepaid interest, called points, when making these loans. You have to compare the cost of these charges with the benefits of the lower payments.

For example, if your payments would be $100 a month lower for the first five years, but the lender wanted an up-front charge of $4,000, you would be better off keeping the $4,000 in your bank account and making the higher payments. Keep in mind, the lower payments don't necessarily equate with lower interest charges. If your payment is less than the monthly interest charge, the difference is being added to your loan each month. The $100 a month is not a savings for you, as you will repay it eventually. It is an advantage to you as it is always better to negotiate to make any payment later rather than sooner.

3. The Collateral for the Loan. The security you pledge for a loan when you borrow is called collateral. Properties differ in their value as collateral in two ways.

One way is their liquidity, or the ability to sell the property quickly for near market value. Any property can be sold in one day; the procedure is called an auction. However, some properties will bring only a small fraction of their value at an auction, while others will sell for nearly their full value. A well-maintained, well-designed and well-built house in a desirable location will bring the highest percentage of value. An unimproved parcel of land or management-intensive property will bring the lowest percentage. Properties that are liquid make better collateral and command better loan terms as lenders recognize that these loans are safer.

The second factor that sets properties apart from one another is that some collateral produces income and increases in value. A good example is investment real estate. Other collateral, like a new car, does neither. Lenders prefer the appreciating, income-producing collateral, and will often lend money on better terms (longer terms) and at lower interest rates when this kind of collateral is offered. Car dealers regularly lower interest rates as an incentive to make sales. Don't confuse these artificially low rates with the rates a bank will charge you.

When you have a loan secured by a property that is producing most or all of the income it takes to make the payments on a loan, and it is appreciating in value, you will rarely, if ever, worry about it. It is safe debt. However, if you borrow to buy an asset that produces no income, like the house you live in or a parcel of land, then, although the debt may be well secured, it requires you to make payments, and perhaps lose sleep.

Set a goal to have debt that is self-liquidating, secured by property that will pay for itself. Owning a house that is paid for and having no personal debt may not cure all insomnia, but it's a great start!

4. Interest Rate. Obviously a lower interest rate is better. Often you have to choose between a lower rate and a longer term. Typically a longer-term loan will have a slightly higher interest rate than a short-term loan.

The important question to answer is: "How long will I keep this loan?" If your plan is to sell or refinance the property in five years or less, then get the lowest-interest, lowest-up-front-cost loan that you can negotiate. If your plan is to hold the property indefinitely (my plan—never sell a good profitable property), then the longer-term loan will be less costly in the long run, especially if the interest rate on the loan is relatively low.

Interest rates on long-term loans secured by real estate have ranged from about 5% to about 14% over the last 50 years. They have spiked higher, but few people have had to borrow on long-term loans at rates above 14%. When we near the low end of this range, then it is to your advantage to borrow with a long-term fixed-rate loan. When rates are higher, then a cheaper, shorter-term loan is better, because you will probably refinance at a lower rate within 5 years.

Figure 5–1 shows the 30-year conventional mortgage rate between 1971 and 2007.

5. Liability. Whenever you borrow money you have the obligation to repay it. If you borrow from a friend and agree to repay it next week, even if you did not write it down, you still have an obligation to repay.

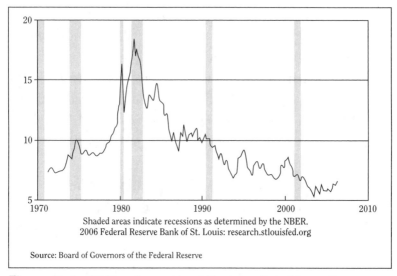

Shaded areas indicate recessions as determined by the NBER.
2006 Federal Reserve Bank of St. Louis: research.stlouisfed.org

Source: Board of Governors of the Federal Reserve

Figure 5–1   30-Year Conventional Mortgage Rate (Percent)

There are moral obligations and there are legal obligations. Liability is the legal responsibility to repay a debt. You can negotiate different levels of liability when you borrow. When you borrow a large amount, your liability, or legal responsibility to repay, is both negotiable and very important to you.

When you agree to repay a debt secured by real estate, you will sign two loan documents. These can exist separately or can be combined into one document. One of these documents is, typically, called a promissory note, and it will detail the terms of your agreement to repay the note. It will state the interest rate and how it will be calculated, your monthly payments and late fees if applicable, and it will address your liability.

The second instrument is a security agreement, and with real estate it is either a mortgage or a deed of trust, depending on the state law.

You should read both documents before you sign them. This may take you a while, so request copies of these documents along with all other closing documents at least a day before you close, so you or your attorney can read them carefully.

Setting Your Strategy for Buying in a Changing Market

The language in the promissory note will determine your liability for the debt. Most institutional documents heavily favor the lender. Millions of borrowers sign them each year (without reading them), and put all of their assets at risk.

You have other options. *Over the last 35 years, I have never once gone to a bank for financing to buy a house. Every loan was from a seller or another investor.*

One of the best approaches is to ask the seller to finance the purchase of the house that you are buying. When you do this, the debt you owe the seller is called a "purchase money" debt, and your liability may be limited to the property that you are buying. This varies from state to state so check on it with your attorney. If you cannot repay the debt, you may have the option of giving the seller his property back and have no further liability for the debt.

If you borrow the money from a bank to buy the same house, it is not a purchase-money loan. If you cannot repay the bank, the banker will hire an attorney to collect the money and you will be responsible for the attorney's fees, all late fees, and back interest. If at a foreclosure sale the property sells for less than the total of what you owe, the bank will then attach other assets that you own (other real estate, bank accounts, perhaps your vehicle or personal property) and then sell them to pay off what you still owe plus all the accumulated expenses.

Another option is to borrow from another investor in your town. Find an investor who understands real estate and who has accumulated significant wealth, and ask if he or she would finance your purchase of a property. Investors who made their money in real estate will be comfortable with real estate as collateral, and would rather loan you money at 8% interest than have it in the bank earning only 4%. You may pay a higher interest rate when borrowing from an investor, but it is worth it, because you will be able to borrow and close faster and with fewer costs than when you deal with a bank.

When you borrow from an investor, you can do so without personal liability if your promissory note contains an "exculpatory clause" that does not require you to personally repay the debt. This states that the property will be the sole security for the debt and that the lender can look only to the property as security for the debt. A competent real estate attorney or title office will be familiar with this language. The borrower and lender both must agree to these terms.

6. *The Debt-to-Value Ratio.* The amount that you borrow impacts your risk. Any property has a "quick sale" price. That would be the price you could sell for in 60 days or less. It will vary with the market, but in a normal, fairly balanced market, an attractive, moderately priced, well-located house would sell for between 85% and 90% of its retail value in 60 days. A harder-to-sell property, like a condominium or duplex or small apartment building, may bring between 75% and 85% of its value, and unimproved land may bring only 60% to 70% of its value.

When you borrow more than the quick-sale price, you are taking a higher risk. Learn to buy properties at or below the quick-sale price. Then, even when you borrow 100% of your purchase price, you will always be able to sell for at least the amount that you owe.

Taking Title "Subject to the Existing Debt"

When you take title to a property subject to an existing loan and do not sign an agreement with the bank to personally guarantee to pay that debt, then you have no personal liability for that debt. If you cannot repay it, you would lose your equity in the property, but the bank would not be able to attach your other property and sell it to satisfy the debt.

Bank loans nearly always require personal guarantees. If you are going to borrow from banks to buy property, borrow only against property that will pay for itself.

6

Nine Ways to Protect Yourself in a Changing Market

Here are some protection strategies your should use.

1. Stay in Touch with the Market

Know your housing market—not your whole town, but the market on the streets where you want to buy property. If you want to buy just one house this year, you need to learn about only a few streets. If your goals are more ambitious, then you need to work to learn about the market on more streets and in different neighborhoods

You can diversify your investments, increase your potential returns and reduce your risk by buying in different neighborhoods. Some neighborhoods appreciate more than others. Some attract better tenants. Walk the streets of your town until you find locations that you are confident will make great investments.

The best neighborhoods in your town will remain popular, even in a down market. There is typically less turnover in those neighborhoods, so prices tend to be more stable. The most expensive neighborhoods are not necessarily the "best," and, of course, whatever you buy for an investment needs to be a house that you can afford to hold until you realize the profit you want from it.

Using the example in the previous chapter of a house worth between $225,000 and $250,000 that rents for between $1,400 and $1,600 a month, you can see the range of cash flow you might expect from a rental house. If you are willing to wait longer, you can often command a higher price or higher rent. However, when renting, it is often wiser to rent a house sooner to a good tenant at lower rent, to avoid a longer vacancy.

If a house worth $225,000 produced $1,400 a month in gross rent, in most markets $400 of that would pay the taxes, insurance, and maintenance. Use real numbers based on costs in your town to calculate your gross and net rental income. A net income of $12,000 on a $225,000 investment would pay you between 5% and 6%. If you borrow money to buy this investment house, your return after debt service will vary based on the terms of the loan. The more you borrow, the less you will have in cash flow.

A buyer who does not need cash flow from an investment might buy a more expensive property, if that buyer could get it at a bigger discount. Although many investors buy houses for cash flow and potential appreciation, others buy only for appreciation. If you have a job that pays you more than you need to live on, or if you have other investments that produce more profits than you need to live on, you don't need more cash flow. Additional cash flow to someone who does not need it usually just produces a larger taxable income, resulting in more taxes to pay.

If you don't need the income from a house, then you are not limited by the price of the house. If you want a house to produce a higher income, then buy a less expensive house to rent.

Capital gains are taxed at a much lower rate than rents, interest, and earned income. A capital gain can result from appreciation. It

can also be created when you buy a property at
When you buy a house at $100,000 below the m
today on that profit, and if you hold the hot
qualify for a capital gain, you will pay tax at the low cap.

If your plan is to make the largest capital-gain profit, then your strategy will be different from that of an investor who is more focused on the monthly rental-income. You can make a large capital gain when you buy, a "going-in profit," by targeting more expensive houses and making offers only to sellers who really want to sell.

More expensive houses often sell at greater discounts, especially in a slow, or soft, market. Look at Table 6–1 for an example of prices and offers in a soft real estate market with this range of properties available. If you live in a market with more or less expensive homes, the numbers may vary, but the principle is still valid.

If you don't think these numbers are real, I want to remind you of the house that Donald Trump bought here in Florida (without asking my permission) for about $3 million under the market. He made $3 million on one house and did not have to pay a dime in taxes. He's made more on bigger deals, but he understands this principle and has used it wisely.

Table 6–1 Price and Offer in a Soft Real Estate Market

Retail House Price	Offer in a Soft Market	Going-in Profit
$100,000	$75,000	$25,000
$200,000	$160,000	$40,000
$300,000	$220,000	$80,000
$400,000	$300,000	$100,000
$500,000	$375,000	$125,000
$600,000	$450,000	$150,000
$800,000	$500,000	$300,000
$1,000,000	$600,000	$400,000

As the price of a house goes up, the risk goes up along with the carrying costs. It costs a lot more to own an $800,000 house, which you probably would not rent, than a much less expensive house that would be reasonable to rent. On the more expensive house, your profit will come only because you negotiated a discount when you bought. You may have to hold it quite a while to realize any appreciation in a soft market.

There are investors who prefer the more expensive houses for several reasons. One is the greater profit potential with each deal. You would have to buy eight $100,000 houses, according to Table 6–1 to make a $200,000 profit, while buying two $400,000 houses or one $800,000 house would give you the same or greater potential profit.

Note that I say "potential," because you don't get paid when you buy the house, but when you sell it. If you can rent a house for a reasonable amount, it allows you to hold on to the house longer, increasing the chances that you will make a large profit. When you buy a more expensive house, you need deeper pockets, so that the holding costs don't force you to sell before you can realize a profit. Be aware that, as you buy more expensive houses, you will be negotiating with more savvy buyers.

You have to be a much better negotiator to make a profit on a million-dollar house, than you do when you buy a $100,000 house. The ultimate user of the $100,000 house is just happy to have a place to live, where the buyer of the million-dollar house has many other choices and will likely be a pickier buyer.

2. Avoid Speculation with Money That You Can't Afford to Lose

A good rule to follow in investing is: "Never lose your capital."

It sounds simplistic, but many buyers will be lured by the prospect of large potential profits and buy property that they cannot afford to hold.

Nine Ways to Protect Yourself in a Changing Market

Those buyers may then become victims themselves, and may ruin their good credit along the way if they lose the property in foreclosure.

Recently, I was offered a house appraised at $1.6 million for $940,000. That may look like a great deal if you just focus on the potential profit. The question you need to ask is: How much will it cost to hold on to this house each month, and can I afford to do this indefinitely until I can actually sell it for something near the appraised price?

Of course, I would first look long and hard at the appraisal to see if it actually reflected current values. Assuming that it is really worth $1.6 million and you can buy it for $940,000 by just taking over the existing loans of $940,000, how much more cash should you have on hand to take this risk?

The monthly principal and interest payments are $5,942. The taxes are about $2,000 a month and the insurance is $1,000 a month. The upkeep on the yard and pool will cost another $400 a month, and the utility bills will be about $200 a month. If nothing breaks, it will cost about $9,542 per month. Rounded off, it would cost $10,000 a month to hold this house.

Mathematically, it looks like a good deal if you project that you could sell it within the first three years. You would invest $360,000 over three years, and if you sold it for $1.6 million you would make a $300,000 profit on your $360,000 investment. That's an 83% return in three years, far better than most investors ever make. If you sell it sooner, the numbers get better yet. If you sell it the first year, you only invest $120,000 and could make a $540,000 profit—a 450% return.

But this is not a math problem; it's the real world. Buyers may not pay you the appraised price, and unless you're a financial superman, you will naturally become more anxious about this deal with every passing month. A buyer may notice that you just bought the house and offer you far less than the appraisal. Buyers of $1.6 million houses tend to be better-than-average negotiators.

Unless you have at least $360,000 that you can dedicate to holding this property until it sells at the optimal price, you would be taking an extraordinary risk buying it.

3. Make the Same Profit with Less Risk

There are ways to take a limited risk on a property that is too expensive for you to hold. One approach is to sign a contract to buy the property with a clause that releases you from the contract if something does not happen. For example, you can offer to buy a house subject to being able to obtain a loan. If you cannot qualify for a loan, then you could cancel the contract without further liability.

Another common offer is to close subject to selling your house (it could be a rental house or your home). If you cannot sell, you would not have to close.

It is unethical to use this type of an offer to tie up a property that you have no intention of buying. But if you do want to buy it, this gives you the ability to lock in the price for a period of time, without obligating yourself to make the payments or close on the house. If you cannot get the financing that you specified in the contract, or cannot sell your house, you can walk away without losing a dime.

A third approach would require you to make a cash investment. It is a contract that gives you the option to buy the property at a specified price. You could offer to make the seller's house payments for the next six months if the seller would sign a contract giving you the option to buy the house during that period at a price. Your purchase price could be the loan balance, plus a small amount to cover the closing costs.

An option contract allows you to control the property with the right to resell it during the six months, for a limited investment. If you have not sold it in six months, you can walk away without any further obligation. You might even be able to negotiate an extension if you decide that the risk of making more payments is worth the potential profit.

Of course, these ideas work with any priced house. The $10,000-per-month payment amplifies the risk so that it gets your attention. The same math and same risk principles apply to a $100,000, $300,000, or $500,000 house. Don't fall to the temptation of a potentially large profit unless you have the holding power to wait a reasonable time to sell and make that profit.

4. Avoid Liability If You Borrow to Speculate

In the above example, we "took over" the existing loans to buy an investment house. When you buy a house with one or more existing loans or liens recorded against the house, the seller does not have to pay off those loans before transferring the title to you. He could deed you the house with all of those loans and liens in place and you could take title "subject to" those loans.

In most residential transactions, the existing loans are paid off at closing and the buyer obtains a new loan. Getting a new loan is expensive, and can be time-consuming.

Some sellers are under a lot of pressure to sell in a hurry and cannot wait for a buyer to get a new loan. This limits them to buyers who have enough cash in the bank to buy their house, and that is a very limited market.

An alternative is to go ahead and close with the existing loans in place, and to deal with the lenders and any lien holders later. If you are buying a house with the intention of reselling it for a quick profit, then most lenders will wait for their money until you resell, especially if you keep the payments current.

In a changing market, where prices may be dropping and the sales volume is much lower, lenders become remarkably more cooperative. Lenders do not want to become property owners.

There are many reasons that lenders want to avoid taking title to real estate, but the two main ones are the liability incurred by becoming an owner, and the negative effect this has on their balance sheet. When a bank forecloses, it is investing in a nonproductive, illiquid asset. The cash-eating house has replaced a cash-producing loan. Their funds are tied up in the last place they want them to be.

Therefore, if you buy a house from a seller who is having trouble making her payments, the lender knows the seller is in trouble and that there's a potential foreclosure looming. If a new buyer will agree to begin making the payments, the bank will often let her take over the existing loan without applying for or getting an expensive, new loan.

If you simply begin making the payments on the seller's old loan, and you have not signed any new loan documents, then you have no personal liability to repay that loan. If you stop making payments, the lender would foreclose and you would lose any equity that you had in the property.

Never buy a house unless you can afford to make the payments. In 35 years of buying houses, many from sellers that were behind in their payments, I have never bought a house and then not made the payments. Make sure you have the financial resources to make the payments or don't buy the house. If you don't make the payments, then the seller's credit will be damaged if there is a foreclosure. If the worst happens and you buy a house and cannot afford to make the payments, offer it back to the seller, rather than letting it go into foreclosure. Your credit and your reputation will follow you forever. Work hard to keep both exceptional.

5. Have a Primary and a Secondary Plan for Repaying Your Debt

Borrowing money in a changing market is more exciting and more risky than borrowing money in a stable market. When your ability to sell a property is less predictable, then your plan to repay your loans is more important than ever.

If you are buying a house as a long-term investment, then the primary source of repaying your loan will be the income that the house produces in rents. Should the net income from the rent fall below the cost of carrying the house, you need a secondary source of income to fund the house's expenses until it becomes profitable.

One source could be income from your job. Another might be surplus income from another house. A third source may be income from a note or mortgage another person owes you from a previous sale.

It is important, especially if you are just beginning to build your investment portfolio, that you keep a careful watch on your cash flow, and that you make realistic projections of both your income and expenses. If you know you will need more money, the time to line up the loan is before you really need it.

An old joke is that the first rule of banking is: "Never make a loan to someone who needs it." It won't be funny if you are the one who needs the loan.

6. Get Your Credit in Good Shape and Line Up Other Credit Now

Most people can improve their credit score by paying their bills on time and not taking on debt to buy items that don't appreciate. Credit card debt and car loans both are debts incurred to buy toys that are worth less the minute after you buy them. Try to get rid of both types of debt as soon as you are able.

Driving an older car with no car payments is a far better plan than buying a new, rapidly depreciating car every three years. Buying expensive toys on credit or paying for vacations with credit card debt not only causes you to pay a lot of nondeductible interest, but it has a negative effect on your credit. The result is that you will pay higher interest than someone with great credit.

If you own your home, one way to line up credit before you need it is to obtain a home-equity line of credit. Don't use this money to buy toys or take vacations. It's great to do both, but do them with profits you earn, not money that you borrow. Don't risk your family home to invest. Use the home-equity line of credit only as an emergency backup in case you have an unforeseen need for cash.

Another source may be cash you receive from selling all or part of your interest in an investment house that you own. Holding a house that is making money every month, both from rent and appreciation, is a better plan than selling that house. However, if you really need the money, selling just part of your interest in that house may be a better alternative than borrowing. When you borrow, you have to repay the loan. This gives you one more bill to pay next month and has a negative effect on your monthly cash flow.

As an alternative, when you sell part of your interest in one of your investment houses to another investor, you get a check from the investor from the sale and your monthly cash flow will be cut in half.

Most people do not invest in real estate for two reasons. The first is that they don't want to manage tenants. The second is that they don't know how to manage well. If you already own a good house, well financed and rented, you have an asset that other investors would like to own, if they don't have to do any work to own it. They want to remain passive. If you have done all the work to buy and finance it, and are willing to manage it, then you can profit from a partial sale to a passive investor who will not do the work it takes to earn that profit.

7. Avoid Debt That Puts Your Other Assets at Risk

Earlier I covered how to reduce your risk when you borrow money. If you do borrow with a loan that is short-term, or has a high interest rate, or requires a personal guarantee, one high-risk loan will not necessarily put your entire portfolio at risk.

You can diversify risk by having it secured by several properties.

Case Study: Partial
Sale to Another Investor

House You Now Own and Rent

Value:	$275,000
Loan balance:	$175,000
Monthly rent:	$1,600
Monthly payments (including taxes and insurance):	$1,500
Monthly cash flow:	$100

Sell an undivided one-half interest to a passive investor "subject to" the existing loan balance for $50,000.

The investor will now receive one-half the monthly cash flow and the profits on the sale.

If you want to sell at a lower price to give the investor a bargain, you may find it easier to attract investors. If you are a good buyer and can buy 20% or more below the market, you can use this strategy to produce a continuing source of capital for future purchases.

Buying investment-grade houses at discounted prices and then borrowing no more than you paid for the house keeps your debt at a level that should self-liquidate in the event you cannot make your payments.

8. Develop Your Management Skills

When a market changes, opportunities to buy are everywhere. Sometimes it is too easy to buy, but property management does not become easier. In order to make a significant profit on properties that you buy in a slow market, you must hold them until the market rebounds. This may be several years, but the profits that you make will more than compensate you for your effort.

Management does not have to be a bad job. For the last 35 years I have managed all my properties personally. During that time, I have taken many long vacations, I have never worked nights or weekends, and I have never taken phone calls from tenants between 5 p.m. on Friday and 9 a.m. on Monday. I have never unplugged a toilet in a rental house, and do no physical labor on my rentals. I make my money buying, managing, selling, and lending money. I hire someone to do everything else.

You can own and manage properties and have a very good life if you do it right. I have recorded a full-day seminar that will teach you how to manage and it includes all of my forms. It is the most important class you will ever listen to if you want to learn how to manage property. See a full description on my Web site.

9. Follow a Conservative Investment Plan

In my book *Building Wealth One House at a Time*, I outline a plan for accumulating your first million dollars, which I have followed and have presented to my seminar students for more than 30 years. The strategy is to buy one house per year below the market price, finance it so rents produce cash flow, and then to hold on until the first house doubles in value.

Some investors who follow my advice have trouble limiting themselves to one house a year. Moving at a faster pace is safe as long as you have sufficient monthly cash flow to cover your debt. Also, you need to learn to manage well, so your houses stay full with good tenants—tenants who pay on time, take good care of the property, and never call!

Your risk increases as you buy more and buy faster. Keep in mind that it is nearly always easier to buy than to sell. If what you are doing seems too easy, maybe you are doing it wrong. Many would-be investors have gone broke buying too many properties too fast.

Nine Ways to Protect Yourself in a Changing Market

Test the market constantly by making every offer better for yourself than your last one. Ask for a better price, better terms, and offer a lower down payment. If you consciously continue to improve your offers, then you will buy safely, even in a dropping market.

7

Dealing with Changes in Your Finances

According to Yogi Berra, "The future ain't what it used to be."

Balancing Your Long-Term Goals with Your Short-Term Cash Flow Needs

The first step in this process is to assess what funds you need today and what you want tomorrow. Many people set goals for tomorrow that are so out of reach that once the buzz wears off, they fall back into the same old, do-nothing rut. The key to achieving goals is to set goals in which you (and your spouse if you are married) really believe. Buying one house per year that will replace your current income in 10 years or less is an example of a believable goal. Accumulating a million dollars' worth of income-producing assets that will continue to increase in value and produce more income each year is a goal that many of my students have achieved.

Amassing $100 million in five years is a dream, not a goal. Sure, some people do it, but they are lucky or incredibly unique: what they did to obtain the money (win the lottery, invent a software system, etc.) is nearly impossible for a person with normal ability. Besides, what would you do with $100 million?

It's fun to watch lottery winners being interviewed. Some are down-to-earth and plan on keeping their job because they like their work and the people that they work with. They might buy a new truck or take a more expensive vacation this year, but they are not planning on changing their already satisfying life.

Other winners go through the money like they're in a race: drinking $1,000 bottles of champagne, leaving $10,000 tips and buying $250,000 cars. They soon learn that spending money brings little joy, unless you spend it on something meaningful.

What would you do if you had more money? It's a question you need to answer. Unless you have a plan you believe will make you more money, you will not put in the time it takes to learn what you need to know to make the money in the first place.

Do you have the income you need to both live and begin to invest today? To be an investor you need your personal finances in order: more income than your current expenses and a little cash in the bank. You can buy a house with *Nothing Down*; in fact, one of my students, Robert Allen, wrote a good book with that title. However, a house bought with nothing down is unlikely to have much, if any, cash flow. So you will need either some surplus income or some cash in the bank to allocate for expenses not covered by the rent.

How Much Cash Do You Need to Get Started?

How much surplus cash flow or how much cash in the bank do you need to start? You need enough money to cover the payments on the house if it sits empty for a few months, and/or enough to make unbudgeted repairs.

The exact amount you need will depend on the price range of the house that you buy. I advise my students to accumulate the equivalent of six months' rent in the bank before you buy your first house. The good news is that after you buy the first house and rent it to a good tenant, you will quickly develop confidence that you can produce steady income. You will not need to keep six months' rent in the bank for every house you buy; also, you will accumulate equity and your cash flow will increase as your rents increase.

If you do not have any excess monthly cash flow or cash in the bank, *stop reading now* and write down changes in your life you are willing to make so that you can have one or both. It's a simple process: either eliminate expenses until you have a surplus, or earn more income. It's a lot easier and less time-consuming to spend less rather than taking on a second job.

Spend Less, Invest More

As a beginning investor my status car was a surplus postal jeep. It had one seat, so my friends rarely asked me to drive. I'd ride in their new leased BMWs and Mercedes-Benzes, but I was buying houses instead of fancy cars. We rented a house for 10 years before we bought the home we live in today. But when we bought it, we were able to pay cash, so we've never had a house payment. Many people buy a fancy house for the same reasons they lease a fancy car: to impress their friends and to receive immediate gratification.

That expensive house will suck up all of your excess cash for years. Adopt a more conservative lifestyle for a few years and you can build an investment machine that will allow you to enjoy the way of life you want in the future.

Credit as a Substitute for Cash in the Bank

An alternative to cash in the bank is credit that you can access if you have a short-term cash need. A line of credit with a commercial bank or with a private investor fills this need. They are relatively inexpensive, and as you repay it your monthly payment decreases. Of course, you need to repay this loan, so have the monthly cash flow to repay it budgeted before you borrow.

Another source is a home equity loan against your home. Don't use your home equity line for a down payment to buy an investment house. Develop the discipline to save the money you need for a down payment, or learn to buy with nothing down. A market that is not appreciating rapidly will have many nothing-down opportunities. Your job is to choose the right ones.

Vacancies

Vacancies happen. Smart landlords have fewer, because they understand how to stay full. My average tenant stays for more than six years. If you have a management program that nearly eliminates vacancies, then you can focus your energy on buying instead of managing. Before you buy, consider what a great tenant wants in a house. A great tenant wants a house with the following characteristics:

1. Adequate room and storage
2. A decent-sized yard on a safe street
3. Clean and well maintained
4. Surrounded by good neighbors
5. Close to shopping and schools
6. Owned by a good manager
7. A fair rent

Buy a house that fits this description and you can attract tenants that will value your house, and have the potential for staying a long time. My longest-term tenant stayed 27 years. They paid off my loan and for 27 years there was never a day when the house was vacant. Now that's a goal!

Solving Cash Flow Problems

Cash flow problems come from lower-than-projected revenue or higher-than-projected expenses.

Rule 1

Make your projections conservative and allow for some error on both your expenses and income.

If you are a new landlord, budget for one month's vacancy every year, and plug in $1,000 just for miscellaneous expenses. As you get better at selecting and training tenants, you will not have these expenses, but during your first year it's good to be extra conservative.

Occasionally someone will try to sell me an income-producing property, and the only expenses the person shows are taxes and insurance. That does not mean that this is a building where nothing ever breaks. It does mean that they did not fix anything for a year. The next owner will inherit a lot of deferred maintenance.

When you first buy a property, have it professionally inspected. Try to hire an inspector who has construction experience, and who will give you a detailed written report. Then, either get the seller to fix the items needing repair, or negotiate a better price. Then fix everything before you rent it. Now your expenses will be somewhat predictable because the house will be in good shape.

You cannot increase your rents just because you need more cash flow. Some landlords set their rent to match their loan payments. That works if your loan payment just happens to be about the market rent, but your monthly payment may be quite different than the market rent (the rent a qualified tenant will pay). If your rents are higher than those of your competition, your house will sit empty longer. If your house sits empty a whole month because you are trying to charge too much, then you would have been better off renting it the first week for far less money.

Use my strategy of setting rents that meet or beat your competition's; then offer the cleanest, best-looking house in town. Your houses will stay full. When you have an empty house, in addition to not collecting rent, you may be paying for an ad, or to mow the grass or heat the house, plus you have to answer the phone and try to rent the house. Keeping your houses full is the most important thing you can do for your cash flow.

Sell Your Losers

If you find yourself with a house that just will not attract a good tenant, or that requires a lot of maintenance, rather than try to solve the problem, just sell the house and buy a better one.

When you buy a house below the market value and sell it for the market price, you will make a profit. It may be a smaller profit than you would make if you held it for 5 or 10 years, but some houses are too much trouble to hold. Sell properties that consume a lot of your time and money and replace them with better ones as you learn what makes one house better than another.

How to Sell

Even in a buyer's market, you can sell a house if you offer to finance it for a first-time or "move up" buyer. Most homebuyers go to a bank or other lenders to obtain a loan to purchase a house. However, there are many potential buyers who cannot or will not go to a bank to borrow. Probably the most common reason for this is a credit problem.

Millions of Americans have had a foreclosure, bankruptcy, or another credit problem that prevents them from qualifying for a loan today. Others have no credit problems, but do not have enough income, or time on the job, or are self-employed without a track record that a bank will accept.

You can sell to these buyers using a lease option, or owner financing.

There is always a supply of buyers in the market. The secret is knowing how to tap into them. See Chapter 18 on selling, to learn how to sell a house in any market.

Solving a Cash Flow Problem

If you find yourself in a position where the loan payments on one or more of your houses are higher than the rents can repay, you have a couple of options. One is to refinance, if you can borrow on terms that will lower your payments. Be careful not to get a new loan with a variable rate or payment schedule or you may find yourself with the same problem again in a couple of years.

If refinancing is not an option, then *definancing* may be. When you definance, you pay off a loan or part of it by selling part of your interest in your house to another investor.

Case Study: Definancing

Suppose that you own a house worth about $220,000 and encumbered with a $100,000 variable-rate loan that now has payments higher than the rents that the property produces. You approach an investor and offer to sell her a 50 percent interest in your house in return for an amount equal to your loan, and agree to use this money to pay off the loan. Then you would each own a one-half interest in a free-and-clear house. Before the sale, your cash flow was negative each month, and afterward it is positive because you have no loan payments. The investor likes the deal because she was able to buy $110,000 in equity for only $100,000; plus she has you to manage the property. It is a passive investment for her, and she will benefit from half the cash flow and half of the profit when you sell.

This same strategy can be used to pay off only part of the debt on a house. Suppose another $200,000 house had two loans, one for $100,000 and one for $40,000. This $100,000 loan has a low interest rate and low payments, but the second loan of $40,000 has high payments and is causing the problem. To eliminate the second mortgage, you agree to sell an investor one-half interest in the house, subject to the first loan, which will remain on the property. He agrees to pay you $40,000 for an undivided one-half interest, again with the provision that you use the $40,000 to pay off the $40,000 second loan.

After the transaction, you each own one-half of the house with the $100,000 first mortgage still on the property. The investor got a bargain (he paid $40,000 for $50,000 in equity) and you own one-half of a property that makes you money each month instead of all of one that loses money.

You can make investors a better deal than in the example above to entice them to buy into your deal. You can also sell more than a 50% interest to an investor if your loan balance is higher than 50%.

Transitioning from Full-Time Work to Investing

Many people have made the leap from working for others to working for themselves. Fortunately, as a real estate investor, you do not have to immediately devote all your time to investing. You can transition over a number of years from working a full-time job for someone else to being a full-time investor. During this transition period, you can develop the skills that you need to buy, finance, and manage property. Other issues you will need to deal with include insurance, uneven cash flows, and an unstructured workday. It takes discipline and a business plan to be successful as a full-time investor.

Buying real estate requires capital, and before you become a full-time investor, you want to know that you have access to both the capital and the credit that you need to acquire properties.

A student of mine who worked for Delta Airlines, wanted to become a full-time investor. He began buying one house per year, then two, then three, and along the way he ran out of money for the down payments. This forced him to look for investors who would both buy property with him and loan him money to buy property. Today he is a full-time investor, and his early investments have prospered as his skills and knowledge increased.

Short-Term and Long-Term Cash Flow

A real estate investor has two sources of income.

1. Short-term or monthly cash flow from rental or interest income
2. Long-term income from the sale of property

Should you need more money than the monthly income produces, then you can increase your cash flow until you sell, in one of two ways.

The first way is to sell a partial interest in a property to another investor.

The second way is to borrow against the equity in the property that you plan to sell. Proceeds from a loan are tax-free, and when the loan is secured by a growing asset, you are still making money on that asset until you sell. Ideally, you only want to sell property in a hot market, although you can buy good deals in any market.

Following is an example of a five-year segment of a full-time investor's business plan. Before you launch into a full-time investment career, acquire the skills you will need to buy, finance, manage, and sell property.

Case Study: Selling a Partial Interest in a Property to Another Investor

Market value:	$260,000–$285,000
Your purchase price:	$200,000
Your loan at closing:	$160,000
Your down payment:	$40,000
Sell 50% interest to investor based on a price of:	$240,000
Cash due from the investor (subject to the existing loan):	$40,000

By selling the investor a one-half interest in the property at a bargain price, you can recover your down payment and still participate in one-half of the future profits. The investor gets a below-market-price purchase with no effort on his part.

Case Study: Borrowing against Your Equity

Market value:	$260,000–$285,000
Your purchase price:	$200,000
Your loan at closing:	$160,000
Your down payment:	$40,000
Borrow from an investor:	$40,000

The loan could be secured by a second mortgage at a higher-than-market interest rate, but with no payments until the house is sold. This would again allow you to recover your down payment, repaying the investor when you sell the property. Be careful not to obligate yourself to payments unless you are certain that you can make them.

Five-Year Business Plan: Full-Time Investor

Year One: Acquire three houses

- Income from rentals $300 per month; $3,600 per year
- Additional income from loan against houses $30,000

Year Two: Acquire three houses

- Total income from 6 rentals $600 per month; $7,200 per year
- Additional income from loan $30,000

Year Three: Acquire three houses

- Total income from rentals $900 month; $10,800 a year
- Additional income from loan $25,000

Year Four: Acquire three houses

- Total income from houses $1,200 per month; $14,400 per year
- Additional income from loan $25,000

Year Five: Sell two houses, acquire three houses

- Total income from houses $1,300 per month; $15,600 per year
- Profits from sales $200,000 – $110,000 in loans = $90,000

At the end of the fifth year, this investor owns 13 houses, the 15 that were acquired, less the 2 he sold in year five. He was wise enough and clever enough to borrow the money for the cash flow he needed to be able to hold on until the market rebounded and he could begin selling for significant profits.

This is the plan I used for the first five years I invested. I borrowed from the same investors who funded the down payment on the property we bought together. They were happy that I spent all my time looking for good deals, so they willingly loaned me the money I needed to survive until the market turned around and we were able to sell for large profits.

Transitioning from Investing to Retirement

Another point of change in your financial life is when you decide to stop actively acquiring and managing your own property. One attractive part of being an investor in the real estate business is that no one can fire you. However, at some point most investors are going to turn the management of their properties over to someone else, or simply sell the properties. Finding a competent manager is challenging. Managing property for someone else simply does not pay enough to attract highly skilled people to the profession. A good manager will acquire property of his or her own.

Another choice is to simply sell your property and enjoy spending your money. Later in this book you will learn different ways to sell.

8

Things That You Can Control and Change

There are ten factors that you can readily control and change.

1. The Amount of Property That You Own

The amount of property that you own determines your exposure, both good and bad, to the market. When prices are going up, you want a lot of exposure. As it is nearly impossible to predict changes in the market, a wise long-term strategy is to add to your portfolio strong properties when you are in a buyer's market, and to sell your weakest properties when we have a seller's market. By adopting this strategy, you will always be in the market, but you will continue to improve your holdings so that you will be safe in any market and can benefit from upswings.

You are more likely to go broke from buying too much property, than to become or remain poor from not buying enough.

Buying real estate is like eating good popcorn: it's hard to quit once you get started.

Keep in mind that it is nearly always easier to buy than to sell. When you are young (or young in terms of your real estate experience) you are likely to overbuy—be careful!

You can buy faster than you can learn to manage. A student left my seminar, excited with a head full of ideas of how to buy property: he bought 100 houses during the next (his first) year. The second year he tried to become a good manager, but the challenge was too great and he eventually lost most of the houses that he had purchased. Buying one house at a time will keep you from making this mistake.

Some gurus will advise you to just buy and hold during the boom times, and get out the rest of the time. Like Will Rogers said, "Buy before it goes up and if it doesn't go up, don't buy it."

My strategy is to buy properties that will be good investments without appreciation, and then hold them through the bonus years. Then, I continue to hold them until I have a good reason to sell. I have owned some properties for more than 30 years. During that time, those properties have increased in value more than 10 times. I intend to hold them another 30 years and collect another tenfold profit.

2. The Type of Property That You Own

The type of property that you buy determines the amount of responsibility for management and the amount of risk that you take. You can make money buying any type of property. Every type of property has its own challenges. An average house in an average neighborhood that you rent out and eventually sell to an average family can make you a much higher than average profit. You don't need a high level of skill, nor do you have to take a large risk, to buy and manage a house. You can make more money buying bigger properties, but the level of skill needed to buy the right property, negotiate a good deal, and finance and manage it right are far beyond the levels most of us possess.

Things That You Can Control and Change

When you buy an apartment building or a shopping center, first you need to know what it's worth and if it's a good deal. Some big buildings never make money because of their location or design. Have you ever seen a building that always has vacancies? Are you smart enough to know why?

Suffice it to say that Donald Trump is a better negotiator and knows more about hotels and commercial buildings than you or I do. The good news is that we can choose not to negotiate or compete for tenants with Donald or anyone in his league. Know your abilities. Buy property you know well and can manage. Stay in your league, or invest the time to learn to play with the big boys.

3. The Number of Tenants That You Manage

How many hours per week or per month do you want to dedicate to buying and managing property? Answer that question now, before you buy something.

I started out buying duplexes and apartments. One day, I woke up to the realization that my entire day, every day, was committed to solving tenant problems. I did not like it and decided to find a better way to invest in property. I discovered by accident that a house I bought and rented required hardly any time compared with the apartments. The difference was the people who lived in the house. They did not call me for every little thing, they did not fight with their neighbors, and they even fixed some things that broke, something that would never occur to an apartment tenant. Over the next few years, I traded my apartment building and duplexes for a portfolio of good houses, which I still own. Now instead of spending all of my time managing, I spend a few hours a week managing the same dollar amount of property, but with many fewer tenants and headaches.

Obviously, the more tenants that you manage, the more decisions you will have to make and the more time it will take. What may not be as obvious is that some tenants stay longer than others and some take a lot more hand-holding. Good houses that attract long-term tenants have taken less time to manage than any other property I have owned other than land.

Even land takes a little looking after as people will dump bad things on it, cut down your trees, and the government may even rezone it for "turtles only." In spite of what the TV gurus tell you, all property takes some management. Choose the property that you buy by the number and type of tenants that it will attract.

4. Your Cash Flow

Cash flow in real estate is largely dependent on the type and amount of financing that you have on your property. Any income-producing property, managed well and owned free and clear of debt, will have cash flow. When you borrow against a property, the debt can be the biggest consumer of cash flow.

Lenders recognize this and limit their loans on different types of property. Table 8–1 shows some guidelines, which can differ depending on your credit, the lender, and the credit market.

Not only will the amount of these loans vary, but the interest rates and terms will vary widely. For example, most commercial loans are for a shorter period, 3 to 5 years, while residential loans

Table 8–1   Guideline for Loans by Type of Property

Type of Property	Amount of Loan Available
Owner-occupied single-family residence	97%–100%
Second or vacation home	90%–100%
Investment house	80%
Apartment building, duplexes	75%–80%
Commercial properties	70%–80%
Land	50%

of all types tend to be longer. Forty-year, owner-occupied residential loans are now available.

From a cash flow standpoint, the longer loan will have lower payments, leaving you more cash flow. An interest-only loan is even better, but most interest-only loans are short-term and must be refinanced.

It's Not What You Buy, It's How You Finance It

Some people mistakenly think that the type of property you buy is the main determinant of cash flow, because they compare the gross cash flows of property. A measurement like a gross rent multiplier allows you to compare the amount of gross rent one property produces against another. The amount of gross income a property produces can fool you.

This is not necessarily a measure of the net income a property will produce. Some properties with high gross cash flows actually have very low net cash flows.

I've owned apartments, duplexes, commercial properties, and a motel, and can tell you that although the gross rent is much higher when you rent the property by the day, the net is not. Short-term rentals require a full-time manager and have many more expenses that eat up a large percentage of that gross rent. A property that you rent by the day or even the week is not an investment: it's a job.

Apartments can rent by the week or month and do produce more gross cash flow than houses. What many people do not realize, however, is that about half of a well-managed apartment building's gross cash flow will be used to pay the expenses, like taxes, insurance, and maintenance. Most who buy an apartment building underestimate this cost and assume that nothing will break—a costly wrong assumption. Apartment tenants tend to be rough on property and move often. It is not unusual to have to replace the carpet and repaint an apartment after just six months when a tenant leaves hastily in the middle of the night.

House tenants are not perfect, but they tend to be more stable and do less damage than apartment tenants. As you become a good manager, you will be able to attract and select the best tenants in your town. When you have great tenants, your net income and your cash flow will be higher.

5. The Amount That You Pay When You Buy

Before you make an offer on a property, you are the one who decides how much you are willing to pay to buy that property. The less you like a property, the less you will offer. If you like a house, you will offer more, and might pay too much. A smart seller (or broker) is going to try to get you to like the house so that you will make an offer and pay more.

In a changing market, you always want to offer less than you would normally. You are constantly testing the market to see if prices are dropping, or if they have started up again. An offer that is not accepted does not cost you anything. You can always make a higher offer.

When your offer is accepted, then you know what that house was worth that day. Every time that you have an offer accepted, make some notes about your opinion of the market that day and why you made the offer that you did, and why the seller accepted it. This diary of deals is a financial autobiography and as time passes you can learn if the deal you made was a great deal, or not. Obviously, you want to study your great deals and try to re-create them. Likewise, you will learn which kinds of deals you want to avoid in the future.

6. The Terms When You Borrow

Just as you make the decision to buy, you also make the decision on when and how much to borrow. When interest rates are low and credit is easy to acquire, you want to borrow money to acquire investment properties. As rates rise, you may want to borrow less and finance more of your purchases using another investor's capital, rather than expensive loans.

Always require any lender to provide you with all of the terms of a prospective loan before you pay any fees or sign any documents. Too often the terms of a promised loan change before the closing. This is most likely to happen in a market where interest rates are rising.

Many deals fall apart the day of closing because a lender changes the terms of the loan. As an investor, you should protect yourself when you sign a contract, by making the closing subject to acquiring financing at a specific rate and on terms that make the property affordable to buy. If the lender changes those terms, you want the right to cancel the contract without penalty. You will have to be assertive to enforce your rights as the seller and the lender will not be pleased that you refuse to close, even though it's the lender changing the terms at the last minute.

In summary: Bad terms on a loan can cause any property to have negative cash flow. Don't borrow money to buy an investment property unless you know that the net cash flow from the property will repay the loan, or that you have another source of repayment.

7. Where You Live and Invest

You can make money anywhere investing in real estate. Growing towns typically experience more appreciation than others. Choosing where you will live is one of the most important decisions that you will ever make, along with decisions on marriage, family, and vocation. Don't move somewhere because the real estate market is hot today. Hot markets attract builders, who overbuild them, and they become cool markets. It may take years before they get hot again. Live where you want to and then adapt your investment strategy to your town.

My students live in all 50 states and around the world. All use different strategies to invest. In a stable market, like Louisville, Kentucky, they buy houses at well below market prices and rent them for cash flow, but they don't expect a lot of appreciation. Inflation will change the prices of the houses over 10 years, but builders produce enough of a supply to keep up with the demand so prices are unlikely to shoot through the roof.

In Costa Mesa, California, appreciation of 20% a year is not uncommon. Although years of minus 10% occur occasionally, a rental house that sold for $40,000 in 1976 sells for about $700,000 today. That's an average increase of just over 10% a year compounded for the last 30 years. That house will not produce any cash flow until you pay the loan down to about 50% of value, but you can probably count on 10% appreciation for the next 30 years, as the growth in population will continue to outstrip the supply of houses.

In large markets like Atlanta, Georgia, you have many choices on where and what to buy. Some parts of town have properties that will produce immediate cash flow, while other areas may have much more appreciation.

All of these places are great places to live. Pick where you want to live, and then figure out how to make money in your town.

8. The Number of Hours a Day That You Work

Someone once quipped, "The harder I work, the luckier I get." The truth is that those who work hard and smart are not just lucky. They leave the rest of the pack behind. Twenty percent of real estate agents make 80% of the commissions. Those 20% are not waiting for something to happen; they make things happen every day by making phone calls, knocking on doors, holding open houses, writing letters, presenting offers and going to closings.

However, I cannot tell you that 20% of investors make 80% of the profits. It takes work to find a good deal, buy it, manage it, and the eventually sell it, but it pays very, very well.

9. The Number of New Contacts That You Make Each Day

When asked how I find most of my deals, I answer, "I talk to people." People get into trouble, people talk to other people, and I talk to them. If you want to buy a house, ask everyone that you meet if they want to sell a house. Ask your mailman, ask your barber, ask your neighbors. When you ask, most will laugh and say no, but one person will then tell you about someone they know who wants to sell.

I guarantee you that if you ask a dozen people a day if they want to sell their house, you will find more good deals than you can possibly afford to buy.

10. Your Attitude

Possibly the most important part of investing successfully is the way you approach it. If you start off by thinking, "No one will ever sell me a house at a good price," it will surely be a self-fulfilling prophecy. On the other hand, if you start your day with the thought that somewhere, someone in your town today will make a buyer a great deal on their house, and today it will be you, then you are much more likely to be successful.

Your attitude toward sellers is also important. If you begin looking for bargain properties, you will often deal with sellers in financial trouble. Typically when someone needs to sell in a hurry, it is because that person needs the money or can no longer make the payments. When you find yourself in front of a seller in this situation, the seller needs to know that you care about helping him or her solve the problem. People don't care about what you have to say until they feel that you care.

Building Real Estate Wealth in a Changing Market

You can buy a house from a seller and make a great deal for yourself, and still leave the seller feeling good about the deal. You do this by being respectful, truthful, and by keeping your promises. It's that simple. Of the hundreds of sellers I have purchased from in 35 years, none has been angry at the closing. Most were very thankful, and some even send Christmas cards. They were happy to do business with me, even though I made a good deal on their house. On the day we closed, they wanted my money much more than they wanted their house.

The most reliable way to predict your future is to create it.

—John Schaub

9

Strategies for the Parts of Investing That You Cannot Control

There are six parts of investing that you cannot control.

1. Income Taxes

Taxes are a part of life. As a U.S. citizen who has traveled extensively abroad, I will tell you that our taxes are a small price to pay for doing business in a country that has a stable economy and real estate market. Investors from around the world flock to the United States to buy real estate for that reason. Think about trying to invest in a country with an unstable government or economy with wild swings, such as 300% inflation, and you will see how good we have it. Having said that, although you cannot change the tax law, you can develop a strategy that allows you to make a lot of profit without paying a lot of taxes. Investors in real estate have significant tax advantages.

First, we depreciate any improved property and use the depreciation (an expense on paper only) to offset rental income.

Second, any profits you make after holding a house for a long enough period to qualify for a capital gain are taxed at the lowest possible rate.

Third, you can sell a property you want to get rid of and reinvest in another investment without paying a tax using a tax-deferred exchange.

Fourth, you can buy a property at a below-market price and not pay any tax on your profit until you sell it (and you never have to sell).

And, fifth, but not least, you can borrow against your profits tax-free.

By using a combination of these strategies, you can make large profits tax-free, and if you continue to acquire property, you can use depreciation to shelter a great deal, if not all, of your income. A special section of the tax code allows active investors to offset an unlimited amount of your income with losses from property. Check with your CPA to see if you qualify.

2. Insurance Rates

Property insurance, like taxes, is an inescapable expense for most investors. Lenders require you to have insurance, so if you borrow money to buy property, then self-insurance is not an option. Once you pay off your loans, then you can decide if insurance is a good bet for you. Many landlords keep their insurance costs low by underinsuring properties. If the property loan on a $350,000 house (and lot) is paid down to $150,000, an investor may carry just $150,000 in insurance, although the house may be worth considerably more. The owner is "self-insuring" the difference, assuming part of the risk if the house burns down. This is a reasonable business decision. There is no reason to buy too much insurance, because the insurer will never pay you more than the cost of rebuilding or repairing your house. A lot can't burn down, but some owners buy insurance to cover both the value of the lot and of the house.

3. The Market for Rent and for Sale

You have no control over any market. However, you can know your market and price your properties attractively whether they are for sale or for rent. Trying to get too high a price either selling or renting is a weak strategy. Typically, after a few weeks or months of inactivity at a high price, you will reduce your price to a level where the property will sell or rent. If you had started with the lower price, you could have avoided the months of your property being vacant and saved the additional cost of advertising.

When markets change, most owners and landlords will be slow to reduce their prices. Price your properties aggressively so you generate interest right away. When you buy in a changing market, know that you have to buy at a bargain price so that you can afford to give your buyer or tenant a good deal.

4. The Prime Rate

When interest rates are increasing, it eliminates the number of buyers that can qualify for a loan. This makes selling harder, but improves the rental market. Higher interest rates mean higher monthly loan payments for new buyers. Many would-be buyers will choose to rent instead, and the increased competition for rentals will drive prices up. Be a landlord when rates are rising and your houses will stay full and your rents will increase.

When interest rates begin to fall, know that the buyer's market is near the end. Look for great prices on properties that you can hold for a couple of years until rates fall, and then refinance.

When interest rates are low, dump any weak or management-intensive properties that you have acquired. When rates are low, credit is loose and banks will finance property that they would not finance when rates were high.

5. Inflation

Inflation is a friend to investors who use debt wisely. Inflation reduces the value of a dollar. The effect is that hard assets, like real estate, increase in price with inflation. When you buy these properties and finance them with fixed-rate debt, your payment will remain the same, but your monthly rental income will increase. Then you will be able to repay your debt easily with the additional rental income.

Because a high amount of leverage is easily obtainable when you buy a house, a 10% down payment could earn a 100% return if the property has increased in price because of inflation by just 10%.

Take a $250,000 house that you can buy for $225,000 with $22,500 down. If it increases in price 10% next year it will go up $25,000. Compare that to your $22,500 down payment and assuming a break-even cash flow you have made more than a 100% profit in your first year.

It gets even better: the next year the 10% growth will be on the new price of $275,000 so a 10% increase would be $27,500.

Ten percent would be high for inflation in the United States, although this can happen. The average over the last 50 years has been about 5%. That's not a government number, but calculated by taking the prices of things that you buy every day (like houses) and calculating the rate of annual increase. At 5% compounded annually it takes about 14 years for an item to double in price.

Houses in my town have followed that pattern, although they rarely go up 5% a year. More often they go up 10% a year for a couple of years, then level off for a couple of years, and then they start up again. This stair-step pattern in prices is typical in the single-family market, although not in the commercial or land market, where wilder price swings are the norm.

6. The Prices of Land and Material

As long as government continues to regulate land use and development, prices of developed lots will continue to increase. It's the land under the house that is actually increasing in value. Just buying good lots is a profitable investment. You lose the cash flow that rents produce—but you have no tenants!

Building material prices rise as demand continues to increase for housing worldwide. With a booming population, there is no end in sight to this trend. Inflation adds fuel to the fire, driving prices even higher. In the long run, there is no doubt that both lots and houses will continue to cost more to produce.

Buying well-built houses on good lots in your town is a sure way to profit from this trend.

Don't spend time worrying about things that you cannot control.

10

Twelve Opportunities for Profit in the Changing Market

You need to be alert for opportunities to profit.

1. Speculators with an Empty House

A market with rising house prices attracts speculators that hope to make a quick profit. At first, it looks like every buyer is striking it rich, but when the market surge stops the speculators are stuck with property that they do not want to rent. They want their money back and, hopefully, a profit.

Because an empty house quickly becomes a burden to a speculator, they are open to offers of deals that are not only all-cash. It may take them a while to recognize that the market has changed, but when they do you can buy from them on great terms. Many speculators walk away from large deposits on properties that they have not closed. Often, they never planned to actually close. They hoped to "flip" their contract to another buyer for a profit.

Building Real Estate Wealth in a Changing Market

To find a speculator who owns a house that you might want to buy, begin looking for empty houses in the neighborhoods where you would like to own a house. A speculator will often list with a real estate agent, so agents can be a great source of leads. About half of the properties I buy are through agents, because they are constantly beating the bushes for listings and often find deals that I might not find on my own.

Before you make an offer, determine what amount you can rent the house for, and make your offer based on the amount of loan that the net rent will repay. This may be below what the speculator paid for the house, but make an offer that ensures that you will make a profit.

If the speculator counteroffers at a high price, then you can make another offer asking him to carry a note for the difference between what you are willing to pay today and the price he wants. Here is a negotiation that shows how this type of offer is received.

Case Study: Buying from a Speculator

The house was listed with a broker for $320,000. The house would rent for $1,800 a month and had expenses of about $400 a month, leaving $1,400 a month available for monthly payments.

This monthly amount, $1,400, would repay a 30-year, 6.5% loan of $221,495. I offered the seller $220,000 and he counteroffered $300,000. I showed the broker an income-and-expense projection containing the figures for rental income and expenses, and details showing the amount of the loan.

They (the seller and the agent) understood that this was all the debt this property could support. I agreed to pay the $300,000 if he would accept $220,000 now and a note for $80,000 payable when I sold the house.

The seller countered that he wanted the note paid in five years or less. I countered that I would do that if they reduced the note to $60,000. I contacted an investor who agreed to make the $220,000 loan from his pension plan.

The negotiation for this property teaches a couple of lessons. First, the seller did not get angry when he received a low offer. He really wanted to sell and had no other buyers. He counteroffered, trying to recover more of his money.

Next, although he preferred a cash offer, he really wanted to stop making the payments on this house. He used the $220,000 from the sale to pay off most of his loan, and had to write a check for $40,000 at the closing. Even if he had to borrow this $40,000, he was much happier than owning an empty house on which he owed $260,000.

Closing Statement

Sale price	$280,000
Cash due from buyer	$220,000
Cash due from seller at closing	$220,000
Existing loan balance	$260,000
Net due to seller at closing	<–$40,000>
Note due seller	$60,000

2. Homeowners with Increasing Payments

Many borrowers have loans with payments that increase. As interest rates continue to climb, monthly payments can increase dramatically. If your interest rate increases from 4% to 6% on a 30-year fixed-rate loan, your monthly payment would increase from $1,432.24 to $1,798.65.

Most borrowers qualify for a loan payment based on a percentage of their income, say 25%. They would qualify for this loan with an income of at least $5,728 in monthly income (4 × $1,432).

It is unlikely that their income has now jumped to $7,192 a month, which is four times their new monthly payment (4 × $1,798.65). The bad news for homeowners with payments that increase as rates rise is that interest rates may climb much higher.

A homeowner who is worried about getting behind on her payments may consider borrowing more money to make the payments until the market improves. Borrowing more money when you already have a cash flow dilemma just makes the problem worse as your new payments will be even larger.

The homeowner's best solution is to sell now while she still has some equity in her house and good credit. Then she will be able to purchase a less expensive house that she can afford, or just rent until she is able to buy again.

3. Homeowners in Default on Their Loans

Homeowners will fight to keep their homes. Unfortunately, some will lose their homes in foreclosure. When homeowners who are behind on their payments come to me, I try to give them advice that will help them keep their home. Some people have accumulated other obligations, such as credit card debt or large car payments, which consume so much of their cash flow that they can no longer make all of their payments, so they skip a house payment.

They need to get rid of one or more payments in order to keep their house. Most of these people have cell phones in addition to home phones, premium cable service, and nice cars; plus they are still eating out and shopping. They need to decide what is most important to them, and if it is the house, most people can keep it if they get rid of all the other obligations.

For those homeowners who cannot make it, it is far better for them to sell their house before a foreclosure sale, than to lose it in foreclosure. If they wait for the foreclosure sale, they will have damaged their credit to the point where they will not be able to purchase another house for a long time. Also, every time they borrow money, they will have to pay a premium interest rate. Even their insurance costs will go up, because they are classified as a higher risk. Future employers may check their credit if they are applying for a position that deals with finances.

Another problem they may have is finding a landlord who will rent to them with the bad credit record. Most landlords check the credit of prospective tenants

Making them an offer to buy their house before the sale can solve a serious problem for them. Be careful: do not to confuse charity with business. You may feel sorry for them and if you do, make them a gift. If you buy their house, make your offer low enough so that you know how you will make a profit.

4. Builders with Unsold Inventory

Builders always get caught by changes in the market. Managing their business is like steering an aircraft carrier. It takes a long time to stop or change course. Like an aircraft carrier, a builder gathers momentum in a booming market, building more and more each year. When the market stops, the builder gets stuck with the unsold houses under construction, plus the houses that are sold, but not closed, as buyers back out of contracts. Builders will be quick to drop prices and offer incentives to sell their existing inventory.

Until they can sell something, they cannot borrow more money to build more houses, and that's how they make their living. Some builders have many employees who have nothing to do when the building stops, so the builder is under a lot of pressure to do something fast.

A builder usually borrows money from a bank for the cost of constructing a new house. The loan is called a "construction loan" and is typically for a term of just one year. The construction loan is typically about 80% of the market value of the house. However, a change in the market may result in a drop in prices that would change this ratio. Offer to take over their construction loan, and you may be able to buy a brand-new house at a 20% discount.

The builder will walk away from the profit on this house in order to be able to borrow more money to build another house. Builders, like sharks, need to keep moving to survive.

The lender that has the construction loan would rather lend you the money to buy this house than have the builder owe them construction loans on numerous empty houses. By making you a new loan to replace the construction loan, the lender has diversified its risk, and the builder's cash flow will have improved by his having one less payment to make.

5. An Investor Who Is Not a Good Manager

Many people who get excited and buy houses when the market is going up never take the time to learn to manage. These owners become victims of professional tenants. Attend any gathering of landlords and at least one person will have stories about all the bad tenants she has, the evictions she has suffered through, and the mess that the tenants make out of the houses.

I want to ask, "Who rented to all of these bad tenants?" The answer, of course, is this landlord. She is complaining about the tenants, when the fault really lies with her.

Certainly there are bad tenants, but you don't have to rent to them. In 35 years of managing thousands of tenants, I have had to evict only six, and none in recent memory. Hopefully, I am becoming a better manager and you can too.

When you find an investor who is a poor manager, you do not have to write him a big check to buy his house. In fact, if it is currently rented to a bad tenant, the owner might be so happy to get rid of the tenant that he will nearly give you the house.

Offer to lease the house with an option to buy. The purchase price that you offer should be for a below-market price and the term should be for as long as possible. Ask for five years (or more). The investor bought this house on purpose. He does not need money today, just needs relief from management. If the investor is nervous about your ability to perform, you can offer a small option deposit to increase his comfort. Do not offer to pay a large down payment unless he agrees to drop the price to a wholesale level.

When you buy from an investor using a lease option, the property stays in the investor's name. He or she continues to make the loan payments and pay the taxes and insurance. You send her a monthly rent check and have an attorney prepare an option contract that gives you the exclusive right to buy the property for an agreed-upon period of time. When you send your check to the seller trusting the seller to make the payments you are taking a risk. If the seller has a lot of equity that she will lose if she doesn't make the payments, then it is an acceptable risk. However, if the seller has little equity to lose, then you should make the payments directly to the lender, showing the seller evidence that the payments were made.

6. An Investor Who Is Tired of Managing

This is a different situation from above, because this investor knows how to manage. He has reached a point where he can afford to hire others to manage the property, or just sell out and live happily ever after. Good managers are hard to hire as they soon figure out that the big money is not in managing, but in owning property.

If you can convince the owner of several investment properties that you can do a good job managing, but that you want more than a small commission as compensation, then you may be able to work out an agreement with this owner that would benefit both of you. The owner has enough profit already, but would like more freedom and time to spend his or her accumulated wealth. You are still in the accumulation phase of your life, and are willing to work if you can begin to acquire more property on terms that you can afford.

Ask the owner if he would agree to give you half the future profits that the property produces, if you take over the management and agree to do all of the necessary work. He would retain all of the profits accumulated through today and will receive half of the future profits.

If you can come to an agreement, you can document it by using a lease that requires you to pay the owner a set amount each month and gives you an option to buy an undivided one-half interest in the property at today's price. Because your option is to buy only one-half interest at today's price, the owner will still get the other half of the appreciation.

7. An Out-of-Town Owner

Anyone who has owned a property far from where he or she lives knows what it's like to worry about it and to have everything you do to the property cost more than it would if it was in your town. For years my advice to investors is to buy property only in the town where they live. My counsel is a result of owning property in 10 different states and in many different cities within those states. It is much easier and less worrisome to make money in your town than in some faraway place.

When you find a property that is owned by someone in a faraway place, you know that the owner would be happier without the worry that comes with the ownership. When making an offer to buy such a property, treat the owner as you would a poor manager of property. Make the thrust of your offer relief from the burden and worry of management, but do not offer a lot of cash. The owner's primary motivation is not financial; it is a mental health issue. You can solve the problem by agreeing to take the responsibility for the property and to pay for the owner's equity when you can resell it and make a reasonable profit.

8. A House That Needs Work

All houses need some work. Some are major projects; stay away from them! Leave the big jobs for someone who views fixing things as therapy. Look for houses that need small specific tasks that, when accomplished, will improve the value of the property. My friend Jay DeCima is a master at fixing houses and has written several good books on the subject.

Not all repairs add value to a house. For example, a new roof may cost $5,000, but adds only a few hundred dollars to the appraised value; everyone expects a house to have a good roof. New paint, carpet, and landscaping, however, make a run-down house look young again. These investments will not only more than pay for themselves, they make the house more attractive to a potential buyer.

Look for a seller who will not expend the time and money to make his house look its best (or for those poor souls who, like me, have no clue what color is "in" today). If you have the talent for picking colors that make the house attractive, do it. Otherwise hire a painter (or a decorator) who has good taste and let him or her choose the colors. Use good paint, because it will go on faster and it does make a difference.

Again, you can make an offer to pay the seller for his house after you get it fixed up and are able to sell it at a profit. If your plan is to sell the house quickly, rather than rent it, then negotiate hard on the price. Every dollar you can knock off the price is a dollar in your pocket.

9. Any Lender Not Receiving Payments

When the market changes, interest rates are often on the move, rising or falling. When they rise, higher unemployment frequently occurs as building slows, business in general reacts to higher interest costs, and people begin to guard their cash.

Lenders are constantly monitoring the housing market, and as the economy slows they are quick to notice higher delinquency rates on their loan portfolios. When they see more borrowers falling behind on their payments, the bankers will begin working with those buyers to help them avoid a foreclosure. As I discussed before, lenders don't like to foreclose as it's not only bad for the homeowner, but also bad for business. Instead of receiving payments, they are in the position of paying out the expenses to maintain and sell a property.

When you find yourself negotiating to buy a house when the homeowners are not current on their payment, keep in mind that you may have an opportunity to renegotiate the terms of the loan to perhaps reduce the payments or the interest rate. If your credit is strong, the lender would rather have you making the payments than a homeowner in trouble. It is possible that the lender will make concessions to allow you to take over the homeowner's position.

10. A Lender That Has Foreclosed

A lender that has gone completely through the foreclosure process and is in title to the property is an eager seller. Institutional lenders do not like the liability associated with property ownership and are not in the management business. Regardless of the amount of the loan that was foreclosed, lenders are open to any offers.

They respond well to low offers, when the buyer will agree to take title to the house in "as is" condition and close quickly. These houses are great opportunities for buyers who have the cash on hand to make a low cash offer, or who have the ability to borrow the amount of the purchase price without going through a lengthy loan application process. Lenders regularly take substantial discounts (30% to 40%) for a quick closing.

This is a safer time to buy a property than at the foreclosure sales. When the bank is the owner, you can buy title insurance and have the house inspected. Even if you agree to buy it in "as is" condition, you will know what shape the house will be in when you get possession.

Don't bid at a foreclosure auction unless you are 100% sure of what you are bidding on and the condition of the house. Many foreclosure bidders have lost their money because the foreclosure procedure was flawed and all of the liens were not extinguished. Or they bought a property that needed much more work than they anticipated. When foreclosed owners lose their home, they rarely paint and clean on the way out. They occasionally take everything that they can haul, including the appliances, lighting and plumbing fixtures, and even the cabinets and the furnace or air-conditioner. A stripped and vandalized house is no small project. Be wary of the risks before you bid.

Note: In some states, like Illinois, homeowners who lose their house in a foreclosure have a right of redemption. That is, they can reclaim their home if they can find the funds to pay off the loan and expenses associated with the foreclosure within a certain period of time. Always enlist the services of a knowledgeable real estate attorney when buying a house in foreclosure until you understand the rules in your state.

11. Real Estate Agents with Listings They Can't Sell

I buy at least half of my properties through agents. The best buys I have made were listed properties. Real estate agents spend every day looking at property, and they get paid to bring buyers and sellers together, and negotiate a deal that they both can accept.

In a hot market, agents need sellers to list their property. In a down or changing market, they need buyers. If you are an active buyer, seek out the agents that are working the neighborhoods in which you want to buy.

Agents "farm" neighborhoods. They walk door-to-door handing out refrigerator magnets and calendars trying to make a good impression. They hope someone will call them when they want to buy or sell. Interestingly, most real estate agents don't buy property themselves.

A handful of top agents in any town make most of the money, and they make a lot. They are also busy 24/7 talking to customers and putting deals together, so they have little time to buy property. The other agents are struggling to make ends meet. The point is that neither group is much competition for a good deal. They may call a relative or good friend if they find a good deal, but they will call you if they think you can buy and close quickly.

I once purchased a house through an agent who had the property listed for six months and had not brought the seller even one offer. The seller had owned the property for more than 20 years, and it was worth at least four times what she paid for it. She owned the house free-and-clear, and her motivation to sell was her desire to move closer to her daughter and family who lived in another state. Christmas was coming, and she wanted to be with those grandkids. I made an offer with terms that made the house affordable to me, and I offered to close the sale in one week.

The broker was not wild about the terms, but when he figured out that he would get paid in one week, and that the seller would be able to move in one week and meet her deadline, he become more enthusiastic. He got the contract signed, we closed, and everyone had a good week. We still own that house and it has doubled in value several more times because of its great location.

Real estate agents do not get paid when they list a property, only when they sell one. In fact, a listing that does not sell will cost agents any money they spend to advertise and promote it. Agents have an obligation to the seller to hold open houses and, of course, the seller will be calling them daily to see what they are doing to sell the house.

When a listing in which the agent is heavily invested is about to expire, that agent is motivated to bring the seller some offer, just to show there has been some action on the property. While you may not know that the listing is about to expire, you can typically find out by asking the seller how long the property has been on the market and if it has been listed with the same broker.

When an agent sells the property, the commission is split between the listing and the selling brokers. Then the sales agents split with their broker(s). Salespeople who sell their own listings will typically make twice as much money as those who sell another agent's listing.

When you find a house that you are interested in and it is listed, call the listing agent to see it, and make your offer. Since that salesperson will get both shares of the commission if she sells to you, she will work twice as hard to put a deal together.

Do not form an exclusive relationship with any one agent, unless that one agent is making you a lot of money. Most highly productive agents are too busy to focus on just one client, so you will rarely find a hot agent who will send you a lot of business.

Instead, make a lot of friends in the business and tell them all to call you if they list a house that they need to sell in a hurry. When they call, stop what you were doing and make an offer. Be aware that real estate agents hear this all the time, so it pays to follow up with agents who you know work the neighborhood where you want to buy. Call the ones that you like at least once a month. Buy them a cup of coffee or take them to lunch. An agent that helps you put together just one good deal is worth tens of thousands of dollars to you.

Some agents own their home or another property. When the business is good, they often ramp up, recruiting salesmen, hiring secretaries and other office staff, and renting bigger offices. When the market cools off, their revenue may drop in half overnight. Rather than close their office, they will often sell a property or even their own home to raise the cash to stay in business. Because they have confidence that they can buy back in when sales pick up again, agents can be a good source of a property at a bargain price early in a downturn.

12. Another Investor Who Needs Financing

Once you have accumulated the property you need to meet your long-term goals, you may want to consider becoming a lender. Other investors are often in need of capital for down payments or for the entire purchase price. While this is not an investment for a novice, once you have acquired and managed many properties you will have the skills that you need to be a lender.

The first rule of lending is never make a loan on a property that you would not be willing to own. The second rule is never loan more than you would be willing to pay for the property.

As a successful buyer, you will know what types of property you want to own and how much you would pay for them. These are critical skills for a lender.

Hopefully you will never need to foreclose a loan, but if you did, you would want the end result to be happy for you. Should a borrower quit making payments to you, it will take both time and money to get possession and title to the property. In most states, you will need to hire an attorney and in every state it takes time to complete the foreclosure process.

While lending can increase your cash flow and yield on your investment, it does require skill and patience. Because the cash flow from a loan can be interrupted (when the borrower stops making payments), you should not rely entirely on it for your income. By having a number of loans, you can spread your risk and make your cash flow from your loan portfolio more dependable.

11

Making Offers on Properties with Changing Prices

When a market is changing rapidly in either direction, it's a challenge for buyers, sellers, and appraisers to determine values. Before you make an offer on a house, you must be confident of the value. Appraisers rely on sales figures, and, of course, the sales prices are determined by negotiations between buyers and sellers. When a market is moving up, sellers continually test the market by asking for higher and higher prices. When buyers agree to pay them, the market moves up and gains momentum as more sales are completed. In a market where prices are moving up, the volume is often high so there are a lot of sales to compare.

When a market moves down, the volume of sales typically decreases as sales prices drop. Now buyers are testing the market by making lower and lower offers. When sellers begin to accept the lower offers, prices fall.

Before you make an offer, study the following list to see if you can determine what your market is doing.

The Six Phases of a Changing Market

- The first phase: Denial—sellers are still trying to get the highest prices.

- The second phase: Sellers use more aggressive marketing strategies, such as making price concessions and giveaways. Buyers are bargain seekers.

- The third phase: With further price reduction comes acceptance; prices stabilize.

- The fourth phase: Buyers return to the market.

- The fifth phase: Inventory begins to shrink and buyers begin to compete for properties. Builders ramp up production.

- The sixth phase: There is a return to a seller's market.

Give Yourself a Range

When trying to establish the value of a property, rather than pick one price, pick a range of prices. When a market is moving rapidly in one direction or another, the range will be larger, plus or minus 10%. If the market is flat, then your range can be narrow, plus or minus 5%.

In a rapidly changing market, if you are looking at a house in the $300,000 range, you should know the market well enough to establish that it is worth between $270,000 and $330,000. If you can state that with confidence, then your goal is to buy it below the $270,000 price. You may be willing to pay more if the seller would agree to finance the property on better-than-market terms.

This works in any market. If the market is more stable you may be able to tighten the range on that property: $285,000 to $315,000, for example. You still want to make your offer far enough below the lower range of your price to guarantee you a profit.

When Prices Are Dropping

When prices are dropping, make your first offer 20% below the price that you want.

In a market that is appreciating, buying a property 10% below the market average would give you enough margin to enable you to resell it and recover your money if you changed your mind. When a market is declining, you need to buy farther below the market to have the same margin of safety.

If you are new to the business of buying houses, offering 20% below the price that you are willing to pay may sound harsh. Rest assured, this is a common practice. Be sure not to use the seller's asking price as a guide when making your offer. It may be 20% or more above the market value. The seller won't feel bad if you pay his high price. A seller will not accept your lower offer unless it helps him.

Do not make offers to sellers unless you have some reason to believe they are both ready and likely to accept your offer. If you make below-market offers on 10 randomly selected houses for sale in your town, it is unlikely that any seller will accept.

However, if you carefully select houses on which to make offers, and then research the house and the owner before you make an offer, your chances that your below-market offer will be accepted improves dramatically. Make offers to sellers who need you—who want an offer, and who are able to accept a low offer.

Case Study: Buying from a Longtime Landlord

Yesterday I talked with a seller who has owned a house for 10 years, and has had the same tenant for all 10 years. The tenant just moved and the house needs work. The landlord does not want to fix it up or rent it again.

The house has more than doubled in value since the owner purchased. He wisely did not refinance, so he has lots of equity. He wants to sell the house in "as is" condition. He is a great candidate for a low offer because: (1) he has a significant profit in the property; (2) he has lots of equity, because his loan has been paid down as the property increased in value; (3) he does not want to do the work it would take to market the house at a retail price.

Offer: $10,000 down, payments of $1,100 a month (80% of his current rent) for 10 years with one payment of $220,000 (80% of today's value) in 10 years. If the seller insists on all cash, then lower your asking price. Give the seller a choice of a low all-cash price or a higher price with terms. Both will be good for you.

Case Study: Solving a Cash Flow Problem

Another owner contacted me a few weeks ago with a cash flow problem. Her payments are more than her income. She has borrowed against her house, but now cannot repay the loan. She stands to lose more than $100,000 in equity and her good credit. She needs to sell and to sell quickly while her credit is in good enough shape to buy another property.

A buyer who takes over her loan will lose about $300 a month in the current rental market. If rents increase at 5% a year it will take 5 years before they are high enough to cover the payments. As a conservative estimate, 5 years or 60 months of $300-a-month negative cash flow (actually rents should increase gradually over that time making this loss smaller) would require an investor to invest an additional $18,000 after the down payment. This property is worth between $225,000 and $250,000 today and the loan balance is about $160,000. Offer to buy it for $40,000 over the loan balance, payable $10,000 today and another $30,000 when you sell the property.

Today's value	$260,000–$280,000
Loan balance	$160,000
Purchase today	$10,000 (cash down)
Hold for 60 months	$18,000 (additional cash investment required)
Sell in 60 months	$225,000 (assuming no appreciation)
Due to seller on resale	$30,000 (balance due on contract)
Projected profit	$42,000 (based on low selling price)

All of these numbers are conservative. Hopefully you could sell the property for more than your low estimate of what it is worth today, and possibly you would collect more rent. As you agreed to purchase with a low down payment and paid the seller more only when you sold.

Case Study: Vacant Spec House

A third owner contacted me about a spec house (one he built speculatively with the hopes of reselling it for a profit) on which he was about to close. He is an out-of-town owner and wisely does not want to rent it and manage an out-of-town property. His plan to sell for a profit today won't work because hundreds of other speculators have put their houses on the market, some at a lower price.

The owner just wants out of this deal. He will pay a buyer to close on this house and relieve him of the obligation and burden of this house. He would rather close on the house and take a loss today than perhaps take even a bigger loss later.

Today's value	$275,000–300,000
Purchase contract from builder	$260,000
Deposit with builder (already paid by seller)	$ 26,000
Balance due to close	$234,000
Operating loss if you buy	$300–$400 a month

Assuming a 60-month holding period, the cost to carry this property would be between $18,000 and $24,000. If it could be sold for $275,000 at the end of 5 years, and you want a minimum profit of $40,000, how much could you pay for this house today?

Your minimum profit	$40,000
Your holding cost	$24,000 (the high estimate)
Cash needed to close today	$234,000
Subtotal	$298,000
Probable sales price in 5 years (assuming no appreciation)	$275,000
Difference needed to make this a viable deal for you	$23,000

Offer to buy the house and relieve the seller of the obligation to close if he will pay you $23,000. I have made deals like this and accepted payments from the seller over time. For example, you could allow the seller to pay you $400 a month for 60 months instead of $23,000 today. The $400 a month would compensate you for the loss each month. If the seller chooses this option, have him sign a note and record a mortgage or deed of trust against another property he owns to secure the debt.

Although there are always these types of opportunities to buy, a changing market makes the opportunities potentially more profitable as sellers sometimes exaggerate their potential losses. Start looking for opportunities and you will never be bored again!

Making the Right Offer for Your Market

Your buying strategy will depend on what you think your market will do in the future. Do you live in a market that is declining today because it was overbuilt, but has long-term prospects for more appreciation? Then getting terms that allow you to hold the property for at least five years until the current cycle reverses is more important than buying at a greater discount.

On the other hand, if your town is not growing in population and the prospects for future appreciation are slim, you need to buy even further below the market. My students in towns in the Midwest and Northeast who have stagnant markets often buy properties at 30% and 40% discounts. They do this because they can, and because they cannot count on appreciation for any part of their profits.

You can make as much buying in a flat market as in a hotmarket, the strategy is just different. Instead of buying and holding for appreciation, you buy at a bigger discount, buying your "appreciation" when you close.

In hot, high-growth markets, even good buyers pay nearly retail prices in appreciating markets because the potential of appreciation is almost certain.

Before You Make an Offer, Go See Several Houses That Have Sold in the Same Neighborhood

If a picture is worth a thousand words, actually looking at property that was sold is worth a thousand hours on the Internet searching with Google Earth or Zillow.com. You need to look at numbers, but more important, you need to see, feel, and smell what a house looks like. It is even more important to see in person what the neighborhood looks like. People want to stay home and surf the Web, but looking at pictures on your computer can never replace walking down a street, looking at every house, and talking to the neighbors. You will notice big barking dogs, huge power lines, or a pumping station for the sewer system that you cannot see, hear, or smell on your computer.

One 1,200-square-foot house may be well designed and maintained, while another 1,200-square-foot house on the same street may be a design disaster and need major repairs. Not everyone has good taste. Most of us can't pick a paint color other than off-white. Most people put off fixing things until there is an emergency, until the small roof leak causes the ceiling to fall on top of the TV.

When you actually see the houses that have sold, you can make a good comparison with the house that you are trying to buy or to sell. Now you can tell a seller or buyer about the house down the street that sold, what shape it is in, and why your price on this house is a good deal.

A side benefit of walking streets and looking at houses is that you will often find an empty house that might be an opportunity.

Calculating the Replacement Cost

If no recent sales are available, you can calculate the cost of buying a lot and building a house to get an idea of its replacement cost. Appraisers use a per-square-foot cost of both the lot and house to establish value. A square-footage cost must be adjusted for both objective issues (like age, quality of products used, and craftsmanship) and subjective issues (curb appeal and design). There are caveats to using this method.

Houses can wear out, but don't read that to mean all older houses are less valuable. The condition of an older house will depend on the quality of the original construction and how the house was maintained. A house built 60 or 160 years ago may be better constructed than a new house (in spite of the fact there were no building codes). If it has been well maintained, it may be worth much more per square foot than a new house.

When comparing square-foot cost, consider the difference in the quality of construction. Many moderate houses are built to the standards set by the building department. Although the codes can be stringent, they don't regulate the quality of the materials or finished work. The quality of the windows, fixtures, and flooring, along with the level of worksmanship, has a lot to do with actual value. Adjust your estimate of value based on the quality of the material used and the workmanship.

Some owners overimprove, or spend more money than appropriate when building or remodeling. Putting custom high-end cabinets with granite countertops in a moderately price rental house, when mass-produced cabinets with Formica countertops would be adequate is a waste of money. Even though these items may cost $10,000, their installation does not add $10,000 to the value of the property. The same materials in a more expensive home may add more value than their cost.

A common overimprovement is building too much square footage. If the average house on a street is 1,200 square feet and the owner builds an 1,800-square-foot house, the square footage over the 1,200-square-foot average will not add proportionate value.

Buying a house that is small for a neighborhood, for example an 1,000-square-foot house surrounded by 1,600-square-foot houses, is an opportunity. If you make an addition to the smaller house, you can add more value to the house than the additional cost.

Gauging the Value of the Lot

Determining what a lot is worth can be tricky. In some older neighborhoods, there are no vacant-lot sales. However, if the area is popular, houses may be torn down to allow for new construction. The price paid for the house is just the lot value.

In newer subdivisions, you can find vacant lots. It is likely that the developer will negotiate lower prices with a builder who buys a number of lots. Watch for multiple purchases; you need to understand that these are bargain prices, not reflective of the real value. Just comparing square-footage cost of lots is not helpful without looking at the lot itself. A 10,000-square-foot lot on the side of a hill, or with a gulley running through it, may not even be buildable. When I developed and sold lots, I noticed that some lots sold right away, while others were nearly impossible to sell. Why? It might have been the shape of the lot, the direction it faced, the placement of utilities, or even the neighbors. A lot next to a bright purple house is harder to sell and worth less.

When looking for comparable sales of either houses or lots, ideally you find them in the same neighborhood, but you can often find comparable neighborhoods. By walking the streets where you want to invest, you will be able to determine the neighborhoods that are truly comparable in quality and desirability, not just size and shape.

12

Finding and Buying from Homeowners Who Need to Sell

One challenge in a buyer's market is not to buy too much, too fast. In my first experience in a buyer's market, I overbought and then I was stuck with several properties that were hard to sell. In a buyer's market it is a lot easier to buy than to sell.

You will find many anxious sellers in a buyer's market. Some will ignore the change, or be oblivious to it, and they will still be hoping for a high offer. Learning to sort out the sellers who are fishing for high prices from the ones that need to sell is the key to making good deals. Although I regularly buy property at well below market prices, every seller I buy from is glad to see me and happy to take my money. They are trading a house that is a burden for my cash. Often they think that the market is going to drop further, while I think that 10 years from now it will be substantially higher and I plan on holding until then.

In a Hot Market Every Seller Gets an Offer–Some More than One

My first years in real estate were in a hot seller's market. When I put a property on the market, I knew it would sell, and sell for a high price, and probably sell soon.

When that market turned, and it turned quickly, it was hard to adjust to a market where I might not even get an offer, much less a full-priced offer.

When the Market Turns, Sellers Are Uncertain

Markets change quickly, but it takes longer for sellers to change. Brokers and sellers are the last to recognize and admit that prices are falling. While their neighbors sold their house in 15 days for top dollar, they have had the house on the market for 90 days without an offer, and are unsure of the value of their property.

Many sellers have significant profits in their properties. Some have borrowed against those profits, and some have overborrowed. In a recent article in a local newspaper, there was an example of a man who had bought a house for $129,995 eleven years ago and now owes $332,000 against it. He used the borrowed money to travel and buy a new car, and now is not sure how he will repay the loan, as he is not working full-time. His house is still worth about $400,000, but if he sells, he will not net enough to take another vacation and may have to get a full-time job in order to pay rent on a comparable house. Welcome to the real world.

The lenders are as much at fault as the borrowers. They advertise aggressively and lend aggressively in good times. When the market turns, lenders will take losses on some of these loans, but I doubt that they will give back the commissions or bonuses they gladly took when they made the loans.

Many Listings Expire

To survive in a changing market, real estate agents must know how to sell, not just list. Many agents never sell anything. They just list properties owned by their neighbors and relatives, hoping that someone else will sell them and they will pick up some easy money.

When a seller lists a property that does not sell in 90 or 180 days, there will be receptiveness to lower offers and offers with terms if that seller really needs to sell. Some houses take years to sell.

Sellers Often Overprice Their Houses

The primary reason that a property does not sell is that it is overpriced. Although buyers are not appraisers, they have looked at many other houses and can spot an overpriced house at 30 miles per hour.

However, an overpriced house can be an investment opportunity. Often the house is priced high because the real estate agent agreed to list it for that price. As the agent should know the market, the seller agrees to try for the high price. As time passes, both the agent and seller become more anxious and will often lower the price in steps. Sometimes they drop it below the market value. Even if they are still above the market, make offers on houses that have been on the market for 180 days or more. These sellers (and the agent) are ready for an offer, and the agent will work hard to get the seller to accept it. The agent only gets paid if the house sells. Give her an opportunity to earn a commission—and yourself an opportunity to buy a good investment. Make an offer.

Some Sellers Do Not Get the House in Shape to Sell

Often you will see a house that is not in shape to sell. A cluttered or dirty house, or a house that needs a new roof, paint, or new flooring is just not going to sell as fast as a *well-presented prop-*

erty. As a buyer, you should look for these poorly maintained houses, because most buyers will ignore them. Most buyers do not have the ambition to take on a project. They want a house that they can move into today.

Emptying out and cleaning a house, improving the landscaping, painting, and recarpeting, all add value and make the house attractive to many more people. These are cosmetic improvements.

Other houses need capital improvements, like a new roof, new plumbing, new wiring, a drainfield, or new cabinets, which are often long-term projects requiring a lot of cash and a lot of time to complete. Unfortunately, many of these costly improvements do not add as much value to the house as they cost. While new kitchen and bathroom cabinets often add as much value as they cost, they can cost a lot.

Look for houses that need cosmetic improvements, not major capital improvements. Even better, look for houses that are in good shape, whose owner just needs to sell in a hurry. When a seller gets in a position where she has to sell quickly, she will have to sell at a discount. A normal buyer just can't move fast enough to buy and close on a house in a week or less; some of my best deals have been houses that I bought and closed in less than a week.

In order to buy a house and close it in a week, first you need to know the market. Then you have to have the money to close it, or know where to get it. And last, you need to know how to get the house inspected, the title searched, and the transaction closed in a week. It can be done!

Few Sellers Are Offering Terms

One way to sell a house in any market is to offer it with owner financing. Few sellers understand how to do this or are willing to take the risk involved.

Look for sellers who are advertising terms. Some will advertise a "lease option" or "rent to own." When you find a seller offering terms, let him do most of the talking. Even if you know more about a lease option than the owner does, let the owner explain it to you. Often the more he talks, the better the deal will get.

When you are buying on terms, the length of the terms may be more important that the price. If a seller is asking too much, but will finance it with payments that allow you to rent it for cash flow today, it can still be a great deal.

Some Sellers Moved Away

When the owner lives far away from a property and something breaks or needs attention, he or she has a much bigger problem than an owner who lives in that town. Out of sight, out of mind does not apply when an owner moves 1,000 miles away from a house with a big loan against it. She still has a lot at risk, and very little control. She is at the mercy of the real estate agent and everyone working on the house.

My rule is that the farther a seller is from the property, the more eager she will be to sell and the better the price will be. Look for sellers who have moved far away from their property. They are eager to solve a problem and will pay to do it.

Some Sellers Bought Another House

When sellers buy another house before they sell the first one, they often put themselves in a financially precarious position. Often they borrow against the equity in the old house to buy the new one, so they have two larger loan payments. This type of financial pressure inspires these sellers to just get rid of the old house, even if they take a loss.

When you find an empty house for sale, become a detective. Ask questions about where the sellers moved. Ask if they rented or purchased a new home. Some sellers have a new house under contract, but they cannot close on it until they sell their old house. Although rationally, they should be willing to just stay in the old house until it sells, once they have a contract on the new one, they are more eager to sell and move.

Ask Questions before You Go Look

Before you agree to look at someone's house, either with a real estate agent or by yourself, take the time to ask the seller a few questions. There are literally millions of houses and lots of them are for sale. Unless you have a system to evaluate the potential of those houses, you can waste a lot of time driving to see houses that have little or no potential.

In a seminar I teach twice a year, students learn how to seek the answers to more than 50 questions in order to evaluate the potential of a property and the motivation of the seller. They do all of this before they get in their car to go to meet with the seller.

Ranking the Seller's Motivation and the Feasibility of the House as an Investment

You are looking for a seller who will make you a good deal on a house that you want to buy. When you talk to a seller or an agent, you should ask questions, take notes, and at the end of the conversation assign a rank to both the seller and the property.

If you want to buy a three-bedroom, two-bath home of a certain size and in a certain price range, and located in one of several neighborhoods that you selected, then only properties that meet those criteria will get high marks. If the house is the right size and price, in the right neighborhood, and it's in good shape, you may give it an 8 or 9 on a scale of 1–10.

If you are looking for a motivated seller, then all of the clues in this chapter will help you spot that motivated seller. If the seller is out of town, has bought another house, has had the house for sale for many months and is offering terms, then the seller may rank a 7 or 8 on a scale of 1–10.

Most houses and most sellers will rank lower on your scale. Unless you are bored and gas is cheap, driving to look at a house that you are unlikely to buy is a waste of time and money.

Testing a Seller's Motivation

Sometimes you get a mixed message from sellers. Suppose that they moved to another home, have an empty house that has been for sale for six months, but they are not offering below-market price or any terms. You suspect that they are likely to make someone a good deal, but you want a sign from them before you make an offer.

One way to test them is to ask them to come meet with you, before you see the house. I often meet with sellers in my office before I see their house for two reasons. First, it is very efficient. If they do not want to make me a good deal, then I have wasted only a little time—much less than had I driven to and looked at their house.

Second, it tests their motivation to make a deal. If they come to see me, it's a sign that they really want to sell. You can confirm this with your questions and conversation once you meet with them. If you don't have an office, use an office to which you have access. If you do business with a bank, a title insurance company, or casualty insurance agent, all of these businesses typically have a conference room that they will let you use. If not, perhaps you could meet in their comfortable lobby. Another option would be a coffee shop, but a place of business will look more professional.

Make Them an Offer That Solves Their One Biggest Problem

Before you make an offer on a property, be able to write down the one biggest problem that the seller has. Here are some of the likely problems.

1. An empty house that requires a lot of effort to maintain

2. A house that needs a lot of work
3. A house with big payments
4. A house rented to tenants that are not paying the rent
5. A house occupied by a relative who is not contributing financially
6. A house with payments that they can't afford to make
7. A house with a loan in foreclosure
8. A divorce situation with one spouse in the house and the other making the payments (or not)

There are many other problems sellers have, but you can see that if you were an owner with a problem on the list, you would be motivated to make a buyer a good deal, and get rid of the house.

When you make your offer, focus on solving the one biggest problem. They may have other problems, like unpaid credit card bills, or needing money for retirement or a child's college education, but you only have to solve the one big problem to buy their house.

Many Lookers and Few Buyers in a Buyer's Market

Sellers become frustrated after their perfectly good house sits on the market for months without an offer. Many lookers will invade their house, often criticizing it, and then leave without making an offer.

When you meet them and show serious interest, the sellers may try hard to play it cool, but their eagerness to sell will be apparent.

When you make an offer, they may respond saying that they had a higher offer and turned it down. Ask them if they would take that offer if the buyer would make it again and see how they respond. Often they say that they wished that they had taken it.

When you find a seller who needs to sell and who wants to sell, make them an offer! They are about to make some buyer a good deal.

13

Buying from Other Investors

A hot market attracts many new investors. TV gurus and high-priced, high-pressure direct marketing promoters convince many people who have no real estate experience, skills, or aptitude to give it a try. What could go wrong? Many of these newcomers buy a property for too much money, sign a bad loan, and then rent to tenants who do not pay the rent or take care of the property. A few months of owning a property that is "occupied but not rented" will inspire many of these want-to-be property moguls to bail out.

Unfortunately, if they have paid too much or borrowed too much on bad terms, they will have no equity to sell. Unless they are willing to write a check to pay you to buy their house, there is little reason to buy these properties.

One other solution is to agree to help them on terms that will allow you to make a profit.

Case Study: Buying from an Out-of-Town Investor

Here is a house I bought from an investor who was not only tired of managing, but had moved out of town and was managing from a distance. Long-distance management can be a nightmare.

He purchased this house and leased it to a tenant for $150 a month *less* than his loan payment. The tenants stopped paying the rent and he was several hours away, so getting the tenants to cooperate was difficult.

Because his payments were higher than the income the house produced, the offer I made had to be something other than to take over his payments. Instead of offering to buy the house right away, I offered to lease the house from him for $300 a month *less* than his payments if he would give me a five-year option to buy the property for the price he had paid for it.

I could either begin collecting the rent from these tenants or get rid of them and rent to another family who would pay me enough to make a little extra money each month. Within five years the market should improve enough that I could make a profit by selling the house for more than my option price.

Although the owner did not like the idea of losing $300 a month for five years, it was considerably better than losing $1500 a month (which was the current situation), and a major problem in his life would go away.

Just Make the Problem Go Away

When you buy a house from an investor who has management problems, making the problem go away is worth as much as the financial solution. A tenant problem that you don't know how to solve is like a bad toothache. Everything else in your life may be perfect, but that bad toothache will be all that you can think about.

I advised the owner to talk to his accountant and learn how holding the property for five years would impact his tax return. The monthly loss combined with the depreciation created tax losses that he could write off.

Always Ask, "What Else Do You Own?"

One of my teachers, Warren Harding, was a real estate genius. He taught me to ask any seller with a little equity, "What else do you own?" Sometimes you can buy two properties at the same time and make a good enough deal on the second one to compensate you for buying the first one. Buying two properties at once means twice the risk and twice the work. Don't leap into a deal like this unless you are ready and prepared.

Case Study: Buying Two Houses for the Price of One

One investor purchased a new house at a retail price. He wanted to sell, but was having no success. He also owned another property; it was well located, and since he had owned it for a number of years there was considerable equity. I offered to buy the new house for the loan balance if he would agree to sell me the other property at a discount. He agreed and I was able to buy two good houses, and make my "going-in profit" on the second house.

Table 13–1 shows how it worked.

I paid retail for house No. 1 and as part of a package deal in which I also acquired house No. 2 at a $100,000 discount.

Whenever you buy a property with a loan in place, be very clear about who will be responsible for the loan. If you agree to leave the existing loan on the property, you can take title "subject to" or assume the loan. Both of these ideas were discussed earlier. Understand the difference and be clear in your agreement.

Table 13–1

	House 1	House 2
Value	$350,000	$400,000
Loan balance	$350,000	$250,000
Equity	$0	$150,000
Purchase price	$350,000	$300,000

Case Study: Comparison of a House Bought by a New Investor at a Retail Price and a House Bought by a Wise Investor at a Wholesale Price

As Table 13–2 illustrates, a wise investor knows to borrow with the lowest possible payments today. The lowest payments make it possible to afford to hold the house indefinitely.

Table 13–2   Comparing Home Purchases

	New Investor Purchase	Wise Investor Purchase
House value	$300,000	$300,000
Purchase price	$285,000	$225,000
Loan balance	$260,000	$200,000
Terms	20 years, 6.5%	40 years, 6.5%
Payments	$1,938.49	$1,170.94
Rent	$1,600	$1,600
Net income	$1,200	$1,200
Cash flow	($738.49)	(+$29.36)

Investors Who Have Loans That They Can't Afford

When a new investor buys a house at near a retail price and then borrows most of the purchase price, he will invariably have negative cash flow. The rents from a house will not often cover a high-percentage loan. Wholesale buyers can have cash flow because they buy far below the market and borrow less than what they pay on the longest terms possible. See the case study on page 120.

Your big profits come not from the small amount of rents you will collect for the first few years, but the capital gain you will one day collect if you hold the house until it doubles (or more) in value. Table 13–3 lists some future house values using a 5% annual price increase.

Table 13–3 explains why my seminar is titled "Making it *Big* on Little Deals" and why I am so popular with the students who have followed my advice for the last 30 years. Many of my students began buying houses in the 1970s and 1980s and they still own them. The monthly cash flow becomes more significant over the years as rents increase. However, the big payoff is in appreciation caused by inflation. If you live in a high-growth area like Florida or California, your end results are likely to be much higher than these

Table 13–3   House Prices Showing 5% Annual Appreciation

	House 1	House 2	House 3	House 4
Today's price	$150,000	$300,000	$450,000	$600,000
Price in 5 years	$191,442	$382,884	$574,326	$765,768
Price in 10 years	$244,344	$488,668	$733,002	$977,336
Price in 15 years	$311,839	$626,678	$935,517	$1,247,356
Price in 20 years	$397,994	$795,989	$1,193,983	$1,591,978
Price in 25 years	$504,953	$1,015,906	$1,523,859	$2,031,812
Price in 30 years	$648,229	$1,296,582	$1,944,874	$2,593,165

numbers. My students who began buying in the early 1980s now own 20 or more paid-for houses, which have increased 4 to 10 times in value. If you are starting today, their success should be an encouragement to you.

When you look at Table 13–3, it is obvious that the higher-priced houses produce larger profits in the long run.

Buy a Great Lot, Not a Great House

It is important to remember that *the lot, not the house, goes up in value*. Don't buy a large, expensive house as an investment. It will cost too much to maintain. Buy the best lot that you can afford, with a house that is functional and rentable.

Another point to take from this table is that you do not need to buy many houses to accumulate a significant net worth over time. Some investors begin with the goal of buying dozens or even hundreds of houses. Buying more houses puts your entire portfolio at greater risk. Buy as few as you can to meet your goal. It is always easier to buy one more than to sell one.

Retiring Investors Need Up-and-Coming Investors

When a market has a big run-up, investors nearing retirement age are likely to begin thinking of cashing out. An investor who has accumulated a portfolio of properties probably does not want to list them with a real estate agent and pay a commission. Investors tend to be thrifty and most have sold a few properties over the years and understand that they can net far more by selling the property themselves.

A challenge with selling investment houses is that they are worth more without a tenant in possession. Of course, it takes some time and effort to move tenants out and get the houses in good shape before selling them.

Another problem is that the investor may have a great tenant that he just doesn't want to move out of a house.

A third problem: when the houses sell, what will the investor do with the cash. If an investor had 10 houses worth an average of $250,000, with loans averaging $50,000 per house, he would have $2 million in equity. If he moved the tenants out, fixed up the houses, and sold, he would undoubtedly end up with less money due to the cost of repairs and months on the market without rental income.

Assuming the $2 million is the gain and that the tax rate would be 15%, then $300,000 in tax would be due. That would leave the investor with $1.7 million invested at 4% producing $68,000 annually, before income taxes on the income. (Depreciation that the investor takes may be taxed at a higher rate, so the actual net may be less than $1.7 million.)

If the investor can sell the properties all at once to another investor, he can avoid the hassle of moving out tenants, fixing the houses up, and selling them one at a time; plus he can avoid paying the tax up-front on his gain. He can also keep the full $2 million working.

A solution to all of these problems is to sell the houses with the tenants in place to another investor.

Don't Lower Your Standards to Buy a Group of Houses

A beginning investor should always buy just one house at a time. If you have the experience and financial resources to buy a group of houses, look for another investor who is liquidating her houses. Many investors accumulate a mixed bag of houses. You may be able to buy them all at a bargain price, and sell off the weak ones over a year or two. Carefully consider this type of proposition to make sure that the extra risk and extra work you are taking on is worth the bargains you are getting on the good properties.

Some investors own nothing but junker houses. Avoid these properties, as they are hard to sell to anybody. The banks don't like to make loans on them as few buyers with any credit want to buy them. And the best tenants—the ones you want to live in your houses—don't want to live in those houses.

Case Study: Buying a Portfolio of Houses from an Investor

When you find an investor with a portfolio of houses that you would like to own, here are two offers that you can make that are good for both you and the seller:

Offer 1

Agree to purchase the entire portfolio at one time making the smallest down payment that you can negotiate, and then making monthly payments for a long period of time, providing the investor with a long-term income. The investor can deed the properties to you and you can sign a note and mortgage (or deed of trust) to secure the debt. A good idea when you have a mortgage or deed of trust covering several properties is to build in a release clause in your mortgage that allows you to sell one property and pay off a prorated percentage of the outstanding debt at that time.

If the seller will finance most of the purchase price on terms that allow you to make a small cash flow profit from the beginning, and then finance the property for a long term (at least 10 years), then the purchase price is not as important to you as the terms.

An investor who has owned a number of properties for many years will have a large profit, and if he has not refinanced, a large equity. A seller with a large profit and equity can be easier to negotiate with than one without a profit.

If the selling investor finances her properties for you, then she will be collecting interest on her full $2 million in equity, and you may agree to pay her more interest than a bank would.

Buying from Other Investors

Table 13–4 Comparison of Two Sales

	Sale Through Agent	Sale to Another Investor
Market value	$2,500,000	$2,500,000
Less fix-up costs	$25,000	$0.00
Less holding costs	$25,000	$0.00
Less commissions	$150,000	$0.00
Less taxes	$270,000*	
Net equity after sale	$1,530,000	$2,000,000
Interest earned	$61,200	$120,000
	at 4%	at 6%

*Based on the sales price of $2.5 million, less costs, netting $2.3 million, less 15%; the actual taxes could be higher due to recapture of depreciation.

This interest will be taxed so the net will be lower. In addition to the 6% interest, the loan may include repayment of principal beginning at some point. A clever buyer may negotiate an interest-only loan for the first 10 years with the loan to then amortize over the next 20 years. If this is done, the payments beginning in year 11 would jump from $10,000 a month to $14,328.62 per month for the next 20 years. A seller in his sixties might like this idea, as it would provide him with steady income into his nineties.

Although the $10,000 a month may be a small reduction in income for the seller from the rents, you can show him that it is far more than he would receive by selling and putting the money in the bank or in the stock market where dividends tend to be in the 2% to 3% range. Plus it is a lot safer than the stock market, because he knows the collateral well, and knows that the rents will produce the income to pay the interest.

Offer 2

Lease all the houses an investor owns for one net amount each month. This net amount that you pay them must be less than the gross rents that the properties now produce. You will have expenses that must be paid from the rents, and you should be compensated for the work and risk you are about to take responsibility for.

It is not unusual for a longtime investor to have lower than market rents. As the loans pay down and rents increase over the years, many investors will keep their rents on the low side of the market to encourage their good tenants to stay. This is good strategy, as they are paying their good tenants to take care of their property instead of paying a property manager.

Low Rents Can Signal Opportunity

I have purchased houses from investors who have not raised the rent for 10 years. Needless to say, their tenants were delighted and would rarely call the landlord; they worried that the call might result in a rent increase. Not raising the rents for 10 years is not good management. The landlord is giving away far too much income. Good tenants will stay at a fair rent if you give them a good house.

When you find a landlord who has not raised rents regularly, this mistake on the landlord's part can work to your advantage when making an offer.

Table 13–5 shows another example of how you could structure an offer to buy several houses from a long-term retiring investor.

The net amount available to pay the owner each month is $3,380 ($4,400 – $1,020).

Buying from Other Investors

Table 13–5 House Inventory Owned by a Retiring Investor

	Value	Rent	Original Purchase Price	Loan Balance
House #1	$250,000	$1,100	$50,000	$30,000
House #2	$250,000	$1,100	$50,000	$30,000
House #3	$175,000	$1,000	$30,000	$0.00
House #4	$300,000	$1,200	$80,000	$50,000
Totals	$975,000	$4,400	$180,000	$110,000
Monthly gross rental income				$4,400
Less: 5% vacancy allowance				$220
Maintenance $100 per month per house				$400
Your compensation for managing				$400
Total costs				$1,020

You could offer to pay the owner $3,380 each month, and agree to take responsibility for keeping the houses rented, collecting the rent, and taking care of all maintenance items costing up to $100 each month. Of course, all of these items are negotiable, but using this type of logic when making your offer helps the owner to see that you need to be compensated for both doing the work and spending money to maintain his properties.

The second part of the offer would be an option to buy these properties at today's prices: $975,000 for all four houses, for the term of your lease.

A longer term is better for you (as the buyer) whenever you are purchasing an option to buy a property. Each additional year you can negotiate becomes increasingly valuable. The first year, assuming the property goes up 5% in value, is worth about $50,000. The tenth year on the same option is worth at least twice as much because the property will likely double in price during that 10-year period. I have acquired options to buy property for 20 years and longer. A seller on these terms is thinking of you as a property manager, who has an incentive to do a good job and keep the properties in good shape.

You want to buy from an investor who has a profit and who will have cash flow from the payments that you make him. The owner of the properties listed above is in that position.

Your option price is also negotiable. In a long-term option, you can offer to adjust the price. One simple way to do this is to make your offer to buy the first house sooner, say in five years at today's price, and then adjust the price of the other four houses, buying them over the next six years. Here is what that offer may look like.

Lease all four houses for $3,380 per month for the first five years. For the first five years, you have an option to buy house number 1 for the price of $250,000. At the end of the first five years, the rents are adjusted upward by 10% on the remaining three houses, and you have an option to buy those three houses at these prices and on the schedule shown in Table 13–6.

Of course, all of these terms are negotiable. I suggest that you print out this type of schedule and give it to the owner to help him to think through your offer. It is unlikely that the seller would initiate this type of deal, and seeing it in print will give him a chance to consider the benefits this deal brings him.

Table 13–6

	Price	Term
House #2	$275,000	3 additional years
House #3	$215,000	6 additional years
House #4	$360,000	9 additional years

Buying from Other Investors

This offer is good for the seller for several reasons. Because the owner has no sale in the first five years, he pays no tax and keeps all of his capital invested and earning a return. As the loans continue to be paid down, he benefits, and if for any reason you do not buy the property, he has no expense in order to regain title to the property, as he still owns it.

If he had sold you the same property outright, he would have had to pay taxes, and any subsequent action to repossess the property would require legal fees

Also, the seller continues to receive rental income which may be tax sheltered by any remaining depreciation. He is selling his houses at a retail price without commissions or vacancy expense and without the obligation to make repairs. As you have seen earlier, these can be major expenses when you sell.

I have sold properties using this technique to many first-time homebuyers and some investors. It is also an excellent way to sell an investment house to an adult child. If for some reason the child decides that landlording is not for her, then she can simply stop making payments to you and you have the property back, no muss, no fuss. You would never want to get into a situation where you have to take legal action against a relative to regain title to a property.

Look for opportunities to buy good houses from other investors. It can be a great deal for both of you.

14

Buying Preforeclosures from Owners

When credit is loose, lenders compete to make loans to homeowners and investors; loans that they would not make in normal times. Some of these are high-risk loans that speculators and homeowners will be unable to repay.

Some borrowers who realize that they cannot afford to make the payments will either try to borrow more money to make the payments on their existing loans, or try to sell the house and pay off the loans. Others use the age-old technique of simply ignoring the problem, hoping that it will go away.

Homeowners who are behind on their payments and borrow even more money to make their back payments are just getting into more trouble. This will typically increase their payments and the result will land them deeper in debt. When you find yourself stuck in a deep hole, stop digging.

Instead of borrowing, deciding to sell while they still have some equity is a wise decision. Their lender may even work with them for a few months allowing them to make partial payments (or even no payments) until the property sells. If they can sell, they will avoid ruining their credit and the trauma of a foreclosure and a forced move.

Lenders Do Not Want to Foreclose and Take Title to Real Estate

When a lenders foreclose they have to

1. Write a check for the legal fees and courts costs
2. Write more checks to repair and maintain the house until it sells
3. Write checks to insure the house and pay the taxes
4. Assume the risk of owning an empty house

Although most loans are to institutions with large loan portfolios, some are to private lenders.

Put yourself in the place of a lender who has been collecting payments of $1,000 a month, and then suddenly finds herself faced with owning a house she doesn't want, and writing the checks listed above for tens of thousands of dollars. Wouldn't that lender rather make a deal with the borrower to continue making some payment and taking care of the house, rather than taking over the house? Most lenders would rather make a deal. As a lender, I have extended and renegotiated loan terms rather than taking title to a property I did not want to own.

Even when a lender forecloses, he may not get his money back when he eventually sells the house. Rather than taking the chance of having a loss today, he will often work with owners and with buyers, by allowing existing loans to be assumed and by buyers working with the sellers to solve their problem.

Lenders Become More Flexible As Times Change

Early in a down cycle, lenders are difficult to deal with as they have few borrowers in trouble and own few properties as a result of foreclosures. As the market continues to soften and they have more loan defaults and more foreclosures, they will become more open to discussion. The smart lenders catch on early in the cycle and, by negotiating with existing owners and new buyers, are able to avoid many foreclosures.

Buying from an Owner before the Foreclosure

When you find an owner who is behind in her payments, there may be an opportunity to buy her house at a below-market price and negotiate a great deal with her lender.

The Lifeline of a Foreclosure

When owners first discover that they are unable to afford the payments, they are the only ones that know. It is at this point that they may try to borrow more money or put their house on the market.

Next, the lender will find out if the owner calls or fails to make a payment. At this point, the lender may be willing to allow the borrower to make partial payments or even refinance the loan.

If the payments go unpaid for a number of months, the lender will eventually file a notice of default, and begin a foreclosure action. There are not a prescribed number of months that must elapse before a lender begins foreclosure. Some may begin immediately and others may wait months or even years.

When this action is filed with the court and published in the paper, then it becomes public notice and anyone can find out the owners' names and the address of the property.

Lists of properties in foreclosure are published and sold. Foreclosure Web sites provide this information to their subscribers.

Hundreds, if not thousands, of people will get the names and addresses of these owners and many will send them a letter. Most correspondents are wasting their money, because few of these letters will be read. To make money buying preforeclosures, you need to learn how to locate these sellers before this list is published.

As lenders accumulate more foreclosures, they typically wait longer before they begin to foreclose. It is not unusual to find a loan a full year in default, without a foreclosure being filed. These long delays are opportunities for smart buyers. When you find a lender who has waited a year or more to begin foreclosure, that lender will welcome your offer to renegotiate that loan.

Beware of the Crooks

Unfortunately, a good number of foreclosure buyers are thieves, who will try to bully the sellers into selling the home to them. Some of these buyers will take title to a seller's house, promising to make the loan payments, but then never make a payment. They move in and live free until the lender eventually kicks them out. Or they rent to an unsuspecting tenant, keep the rent, but do not make the payments. This is called "equity skimming" and is illegal. The resulting foreclosure will damage the credit of the sellers, and any tenants will lose their security deposit and be evicted, even though they have paid the rent.

When you make an offer to people facing foreclosure, you can make a significant profit, without taking advantage of them or causing them grief. They need relief from a loan they cannot repay. When you agree to buy their house and repay that loan, have the resources lined up to repay it. Never agree to pay a loan unless you know that you can do so.

The Day of the Foreclosure

Eventually the lender will foreclose if the borrower does not respond to the bank's request for payments. A foreclosure is the process whereby the lender demands the money owed (including any legal fees and money that has been spent protecting the property from damage). After the court has issued a final judgment a trustee or court employee auctions the property. The terms of these auctions vary from state to state, and even county to county. To learn more about these sales and the system in your town, attend several sales. Come early and ask questions of the person conducting the sale. Ask how the auction is conducted, who may bid, how much money you need to pay when you make your bid and how you have to pay for the property if you are the winner. *Don't bid!* Just ask a lot of questions and then watch the show. If you attend a number of foreclosure auctions, in most towns you will often notice some of the same bidders at the sales. They are professional buyers. They may be attorneys or bankers or other investors, but they know more than you do about the process. They may even work together to bid up the price of properties when an outsider (that's you) tries to buy a property. Buying at a foreclosure sale is a high-stakes game and is not for beginning investors.

Often a successful bidder must pay *all cash* the day of the sale, and takes title in "as is" condition. That means there are no guarantees or warrantees of any kind. Because this is a very risky way to buy a property, the bids are typically well below the market price. In the next chapter, I discuss strategies for buying at foreclosure auctions.

A foreclosure can be an opportunity, but most are not. Don't make the mistake of just looking at foreclosed properties. They are often weak properties in bad areas. Look for houses in neighborhoods where you want to buy, and when you find a foreclosure in that neighborhood, be ready to make an offer.

I have purchased houses in the best neighborhoods in our town in foreclosure. Rich people get into trouble too. Often they are easier to buy from, because they are confident that they will soon have the opportunity to buy again. You may want to assist, but not buy from, a newly poor family losing the family home due to some financial tragedy.

Finding Sellers Who Need to Sell–before Your Competition Finds Them

Rather than chasing every foreclosure in your town, first identify which type of property you want to buy; then identify the area of town in which you want to buy; and only then begin looking for opportunities.

The best time to make an offer to a preforeclosure seller is before you have a lot of competition from the many "foreclosure buyers" in your town. Those buyers are alerted to the opportunity when the lender files the foreclosure lawsuit or notice of default. If you find a seller who is behind on his payments before this notice is filed, the chances are good that you will be the only buyer with whom he is dealing.

There are many effective ways to find a seller who may be in foreclosure once you have targeted a neighborhood. The most effective takes a little time and commitment on your part: it is walking through a neighborhood, talking to the neighbors, and asking if they know anyone who wants to sell.

Walking through a neighborhood, not driving your car or even riding your bike: walking is the secret to success. Police have learned that when they "walk a beat," they get to know the people and develop trust and that leads to better communication and safer neighborhoods.

If you drive your car down a street, you will miss a lot of details that you need to notice: the house that needs a paint job; an empty house; people packing to move; and, most importantly, the talkative neighbor who knows everything that's going on in the neighborhood.

In the class I teach twice a year, we walk streets in the town where the class is held and talk to neighbors, simply asking, "Do you know anyone who wants to sell?" You would be amazed how much information the students learn about a neighborhood in just a few hours on the street, and how many opportunities they find.

Like many teenagers, I had a paper route. My job was to walk door-to-door and ask people in my neighborhood to subscribe to the paper. When someone agreed, I would deliver the paper to the house for a week, and then go back and knock on their door again to collect the money for that week. It was time-intensive and not a very efficient way to deliver papers, but it was great training.

What you learn in door-to-door sales of any kind is that most people will talk to you and many will actually buy something from you. The grumpy ones will share a mean word, but you quickly learn to brush off these turkeys and look for the opportunities

If you have sold papers or Girl Scout cookies, or if you have campaigned door-to-door, you know this. If you have not, it is a skill worth acquiring.

Choosing the right neighborhood is the important first step. If you are buying a house for an investment, buy one in a neighborhood where you are comfortable walking the streets and talking to the neighbors. Then when you buy there, you will be comfortable talking to the tenants who want to rent your house.

Another effective method of finding sellers before your competition is mailing letters to all the owners in a neighborhood telling them that you would like to buy a house in that neighborhood. The letter must be sincere and as personal as you can make it. It helps to say that you know their neighborhood (or even their street) and have long wanted to buy there.

Explain that you are not a Realtor (unless you are—then disclose) and tell them that you are willing and able to close quickly.

A short, personalized letter is most likely to be read. You have probably received letters from real estate agents, and perhaps from other buyers, trying to list or buy your home. The next time you receive one of these, start a file and keep the letters. Look for ones that are especially appealing to you and try to mimic them when you send out your letters.

The secret to success when mailing is to target a neighborhood, personalize the letter, and then to mail it to the same people more than once. Persistence pays. Most people will throw away your first letter, and maybe your second one. But when the day comes that they do want to sell, then your letter (maybe your third one, maybe your tenth) may show up the right week and they will know that you must really want to buy their house: you have been writing them letters for months. This gives you a big advantage over your competition, who are generating form post cards or nonpersonalized letters.

Generating leads using mail is a numbers game. If you identify a neighborhood with 500 homes, you know that a certain number of those homeowners will sell each year. If you mail all 500 owners a letter every other month for a year, you will send out 6 letters to all 500 or a total of 3,000 letters. Assuming the letters cost you 50 cents each, that's an investment of $1,500, plus your time. If you buy just one house as a result of those letters, is that a good return on your money and time? Another way to think of it: would you pay someone a $1,500 referral fee if they told you about a house that you could buy at a below-market price?

If you choose to use this technique, be smarter than your competition, who may also be using direct mail. As an owner of multiple properties in many neighborhoods, I get many letters, often from the same buyer. They are obviously not paying any attention to whom they are mailing. If they were paying attention they would not send me five identical letters the same day.

Print out an alphabetized list of the names you plan to mail to and look for duplicate names listed as owners (like me) who own several houses in the neighborhood. Take a different approach with these investors. Contact them and tell them that you noticed that they owned several houses and that you may be interested in buying one or more when they decide to sell.

By printing out and studying these names, and then going further by looking up the owners, finding out when they bought, how much they paid, and even how much they borrowed when they bought, you will begin to "own" this neighborhood. When you walk through the neighborhood, you will begin putting names and addresses together. When an opportunity appears and it will, you will be best prepared to take advantage of it. Luck happens when opportunity meets a prepared buyer. Be prepared and you will get lucky.

To Buy You Have to Talk with the Sellers

An important part of sending out letters is having an easy way for them to call you after they read your letter. Successful buyers often have a phone dedicated only to buying. It is the number they give to potential sellers (but not to everyone else). With cell phones you can have a number that they can call anytime and reach you.

When sellers call you, this is the day and the hour that they have decided to sell their house. Unless you answer, they may not leave a message. If you are handing out business cards with your number on it, or mailing letters, or putting signs up that say you buy houses, the secret to success is answering the phone and talking to a ready seller.

Don't Just Shoot the Breeze, Be Prepared!

When sellers call, you need to be able to ask enough questions both to be able to find them again and to evaluate their situation. The evaluation is to assess whether the sellers are ready to sell today.

By asking the question directly—"How soon do you want to sell?"—you will learn what you need to know. A good follow-up question is "How soon do you want to move?"

You are looking for an answer like "We could be out this weekend," as opposed to "We don't want to move until school is out." Both owners might be behind on their payments, but only one has recognized the seriousness of the problem.

Once you have identified the opportunity, make an appointment to get together. It does not have to be at the owner's house. If this is the owner's home (not an investment property) then ask him or her to meet you at your office or a neutral location to avoid the emotional connection to the house.

Do not make an offer when you first meet the owners. The purpose of that first meeting is to begin to develop trust. Be on time, do everything you say you will do, and set another time to get together. If they are anxious to sell, it could be later that day or the next day. Give yourself enough time to check out values (which you will already have a feel for as it is in "your neighborhood") and to make a list of questions that you will need answered before you can make an offer.

Getting Prepared to Make an Offer to a Preforeclosure Seller

Before you make an offer, you want to learn all you can about the property and the sellers' situation. That includes the details about how much they owe and the identity of the lender. The key words here are "ask" and "verify." Sellers who want to sell you their house may be eager to answer your questions, but they may not know the answers. Even without the information, they may blurt out answers.

Here are a few of my favorite questions.

1. How long have you owned the house?
2. Who are the owners?
3. How much did you pay for it?
4. How much do you owe? To whom? Payments? Terms? Interest rate?
5. Are your payments current?
6. When can you move?
7. Is there anything wrong with your house?

Buying Preforeclosures from Owners

There are a lot of other questions you can and should ask, about ages of appliances, room sizes, schools, utilities, etc., but the list above contains questions that are hard for them to answer. Not because they don't know the answers, but because they don't want you to know the answers.

You will learn a lot, not only from their answers, but how they answer these questions. If they refuse to answer, then they are not quite ready to sell you their house. The problem may be that they don't know you well enough to trust you with these answers yet. If you think this is the problem, slow down and spend more time asking less important questions like "What color is that carpet?" "Are there schools nearby?" "How much is your average electric bill?" "How much do you pay in taxes and insurance?"

After you build up some rapport, work in one of the harder questions and see if they answer. Let them talk—you listen. After you have asked the questions, you will begin to understand their situation and begin formulating an offer that will solve their one major problem.

Verify their answers for two reasons. One reason is to see if they are giving you honest answers. If they are blatantly lying, walk away. You cannot outsmart a crook. Two—you need good information regarding loan balances, payment schedules, insurance and tax bills that have been paid or are due to be paid, etc. Verify by asking for copies of loan statements, insurance policies, tax records, and the title insurance policy indicating when they bought the house (it will have the owners' names, a good legal description, and the purchase price).

Before you make an offer to buy the house, you want the owners to be comfortable with you and feel that you are there to help them solve a problem. Be trustworthy, and ask the questions you need answers to before you can make an offer that does solve their problem.

Have the house inspected after you make your offer, but before you close. The inspection will expose any expensive-to-repair problems. Your contract should allow you to require that the owners fix these items or allow you to walk away from the deal.

If you are new to buying, use a checklist like the one that follows.

Buying and Closing Checklist

1. Identify a potential bargain purchase; ask *the* questions.
2. Write down the one urgent problem you can solve for the seller
3. Establish the fair market value, give or take 5%.
4. Research the market rent and likely net income the property will produce.
5. State your minimum acceptable profit on this house.
6. Formulate an offer that solves the seller's one urgent problem.
7. Make the offer. Insist on either an acceptance or a counter-offer.
8. If your first offer is not accepted, make another offer based on any new information.
9. If the seller is unresponsive, but you remain convinced there is opportunity, go away and come back in a week with another offer.
10. Get the contract accepted—signed by all parties.
11. Make your earnest money deposit (sum paid when you make an offer to your attorney or title agent).
12. Retain a house inspector and termite inspector if needed.
13. Order a title search with a title company, attorney, or escrow company.
14. Talk with the agent or attorney who will prepare the closing documents to alert them to any unusual clauses in the contract.
15. Get copies of any documents you will be required to sign the day before the closing and get a copy of the title insurance commitment—read to check for exceptions.

16. Read closing documents *carefully!*
17. Conduct a walk-through inspection.
18. On the day of closing, review the documents and collect the appropriate documents, instruction manuals, and warranties; get all of the keys and garage door opener.

Note: When you are buying, take your time. Time is on your side.

(The preceding list reprinted by permission: from John Schaub's "Making It Big on Little Deals" Seminar.)

Making the Offer

Making the offer to owners who are at risk for losing their home is different than buying from another seller. The sellers will be in a bigger hurry, and the lender may be a key to making a good deal. In the next chapter you will learn about negotiating with lenders.

When you find an owner who really needs to sell, recognize that he or she is going to make somebody a good deal. It might as well be you.

Each day that sellers who are behind on their payments wait to sell, they are put under more pressure and they get deeper in the hole. A loan in default will often accrue interest at a higher rate, and late fees will add even more to the loan balance each month. On top of that, court costs and attorney or trustee fees will add more to the loan balance.

If the sellers want to walk away with any money, they need to move quickly. Explain this to them.

To calculate what you will offer, start with a range of prices that the house could sell for given a normal amount of time to market it. From that, deduct any costs of repairs, projected holding costs, and the minimum profit that you would want to make on a house in this price range. Table 14–1 shows an example.

Table 14–1

House value	$250,000–$275,000
Repair costs	–$10,000
Holding costs (3 months)	–$4,500
Minimum profit	–$40,000
Maximum offer	$195,500
Existing loan balances	$150,000 (first)
	$25,000 (second)

Your offer could be to pay the sellers $20,000 cash at closing, with the closing contingent upon your ability to assume the existing loans on terms acceptable to you.

You may decide to refinance or bring in an investor to pay off the existing loans, but that would be at your option. Unless you can buy at a bigger discount, you would not want to agree to pay off both loans at closing as that would require another $175,000 in cash.

If you can buy this house for $20,000 down, your projected profit of about $40,000 (with potential of another $25,000 if you can sell for the high side of the range) is adequate compensation for the risk and work involved. If you have to pay $195,000 cash at closing, you will want to make more than a $40,000 profit.

Buying Right Before a Sale (or Even After)

Some people in foreclosure circumstances procrastinate: they fail to make a decision until the final moment. My office was located directly across from the courthouse for 25 years. The courthouse is where all the foreclosure sales are held in my town. It was easy to walk across the street to the sale. It was equally easy for those who were about to lose their house to walk to my office.

Often, owners would come to see me just before the sale, and some after the sale. Under Florida law, the owner still has title to the house until a judge transfers title to the buyer. So I could still buy from the "owner" up to that title transfer. If fact, some states give the owner who loses a property in foreclosure time to reclaim or redeem the property. Don't give these "owners" any money for their title, unless you know that they still own the property and you know of all the encumbrances. This will take the help of a fast-moving and competent real estate attorney. A sharp attorney can do a title search and close a transaction in an hour or two. The challenge is finding one who will drop what she is doing and work now to get the deal closed.

Rights of Redemption

Each state has a different approach to foreclosures and the rights of the (now former) owners after the foreclosure. Many states have no right of redemption, and the owners' rights are extinguished at the sale. Other states allow owners as long as a year to redeem their property by paying the amounts due on the loans, plus costs.

Learn your state law. If your state allows redemption for some period, you may be able to buy those rights from the owner. That would allow you to buy the house and sell to another without waiting for the redemption period to run. Check this out with a real estate attorney in your town.

If you buy a property subject to a right of redemption, you can rent it, but it would be unwise to spend any serious money improving the property until the redemption period expires. Most people never buy back a house they lose in foreclosure, but if you buy one at a large discount, the odds are better that it would be redeemed.

To summarize, find a house in a neighborhood where you want to buy that is owned by a seller who is behind on his payments. Spend time with the owner and ask questions that get you the information you need to make an offer. Make your offer, explaining that the longer the owner waits, the less he will net from the house. Then, after you have a signed contract, contact the lender.

15

A Professional Buyer's Secrets for Negotiating Short Sales and Other Great Deals with Lenders

In 35 years of buying foreclosures, I have made many deals with lenders. The key to making a great deal on a preforeclosure purchase almost always involves the lender. The seller often owes nearly as much as the property is worth, and sometimes more than it is worth. There are many ways that a lender can help you buy a property, when the lender has a loan and is not receiving payments.

Lenders want to get rid of nonperforming loans and any property that they acquire through foreclosure. A bank with a history of making a lot of bad loans will draw the attention of both its stockholders and the Federal Bank Examiners. This is not the kind of attention your local banker wants.

Help Yourself by Helping the Banker

When a lender is owed a certain amount, there is no guarantee that they will receive it. In fact, if a lender forecloses on a loan, she often loses money. The costs of foreclosing, repairing, holding on to the property, and marketing can easily eat up 20% to 30% of the amount of the loan.

This amount that the lender may lose is composed of several elements.

1. The cost of a commission (6%–7%)
2. The average cost of repairs (5%–10%)
3. Court costs and legal fees (4%–6%)
4. The cost of holding, taxes, insurance, and ongoing maintenance (5%–10%)

The lender would much rather be paid off, even at a discount, than foreclose. It's better for the homeowner and for the lender to make a deal before the foreclosure sale. The homeowner may lose his equity, but can avoid the trauma and stigma of a foreclosure.

Who Should You Talk To at the Bank?

One secret to doing business with a lender is to remember that the banker on the other end of the phone gets a lot of calls from people who do not follow through or keep their word. You must first sell yourself to the banker, then sell your offer.

If you develop a good relationship with a banker, you can do repeat business with that banker. The second deal will be easier than the first because he knows that you will perform.

In a smaller community bank, start your discussion with the loan officer who made the loan. You can often find his or her name on the original loan documents, which the sellers will have in their possession. If they can't find the documents, go online or go to the courthouse and look up the original note and mortgage or deed of trust. Look for a signature of a bank officer.

Loan officers have a personal interest in a good resolution of the loan that they make. It does not help their lending credentials if many of their loans go into foreclosure.

A loan officer probably will not have the authority to make a decision, but he can get to the head of the residential lending department at the bank, and she will have the authority. Do your best to meet personally with the decision maker; impress her that you want to help both the bank and the borrower out of a bad situation. If you have good credit, tell her about it. If you have had experiences helping others in foreclosure, tell her. The bank officers want to do business with someone who can perform.

In larger regional banks, there are separate departments, often called loss mitigation departments, established to "work out" problems when borrowers cannot make their payments. When you are talking with the owners, ask them to show you any letters that they have received from the bank. These will often be from a collection or loss mitigation specialist. Note that person's name and phone number.

When Is the Best Time to Contact the Lender?

Approach the lender as soon as you have a contract with the sellers to buy their property. Try to contact the bankers before they start the foreclosure process: before they have paid any legal fees and before anyone else knows about the deal.

The lender will not talk to you about their borrowers' situation, unless you have a contract to buy their house. In addition to the contract, the bank may request an authorization letter from the borrower. It is a simple letter stating that they have agreed to sell you the house and request that the lender cooperate in any way possible, including revealing the loan balances and any other charges that are due.

The exception to this rule is when you approach the bank, not to buy the house, but to buy the loan. A bank can sell a loan at any time. If the loan is nonperforming (the borrowers are behind in their payments), then the bank might sell it at a discount.

Do your best to get to the lender before the lender hires an attorney to foreclose on the property. I have nothing against attorneys. I'm married to a good one. But once the attorneys have the file, they will not be in a hurry to settle. Because they are getting paid by the hour, it's against their self-interest to solve the problem in one hour.

Giving a Bank a Deed in Lieu of Foreclosure

One solution for an owner who can't make his payments is to deed the property to the lender. The lender has to agree to accept the deed (you can't just deed someone a property without their permission), and the title must be free of other encumbrances. If the borrower has placed a second mortgage on the property, or has a lien or judgment against him, then those liens would remain on the property title. In this case the lender will not accept the deed, because a foreclosure suit is still needed to free the property title from the other liens.

When a bank gains title to a property through a deed in lieu of foreclosure, there is no public notice and few people outside of the seller and the bank will know about this transaction. If you are negotiating to buy a house and see that this is a solution, you can help arrange it and at the same time agree to buy the house from the bank. The bank does not want the house; it wants either a performing loan or the money. You can either buy it and finance it from the bank, or if you have another source of funds, negotiate a bargain sale from the bank. Even though the bank does not have the cost of foreclosure, it will still have the other costs associated with holding the property and would rather sell today than hold on to the property.

Many loans are sold by the originating lender. If the loans are sold to another lender, that new lender typically begins servicing the loans, collecting the payments and any required escrow money.

Some loans are sold to large financial services companies like Fannie Mae. When those loans go into default, they are often sold as a package to a financial buyer who specializes in workouts. The federal government originates some loans through the Veterans Administration and insures loans for banks through the FHA (the Federal Housing Administration). Information on homes foreclosed on by the Veterans Administration or FHA is available on the HUD (U.S. Department of Housing and Urban Development) Web site: www.hud.gov.

Understanding the Banking Process

When homeowners are behind on their payments, the loan will be assigned to a specialist in the bank. These are not the same people who make the loans or open accounts at the bank. These are bankers who deal only with borrowers who are behind in their payments. They typically have the authority to negotiate within limits, or can quickly get permission to make a deal with a new buyer.

Most buyers do not try to negotiate better terms on the existing loan; they simply refinance the loan with the same lender or another lender. This is the lender's first preference: when a bank makes a new loan it can charge and collect new fees, application fees, even points. Typically, when you call the bank, they will encourage you to apply for a new loan.

If you do, you will first have to qualify for that loan, and then pay all of the associated closing costs. This is a great deal for the bank, but not a great deal for you.

Rather than getting a new loan, you can ask the lender to do one of two things that are good for you.

1. They could allow you to "take over" (meaning take subject to the loan, as discussed earlier) or assume the existing loan, modifying some of the terms.
2. They could agree to let you pay off the existing loan at a discount. This is commonly referred to as a "short sale" because you buy the property for less than—or "short" of—the loan balance.

Nine Ways Lenders Can Modify an Existing Loan to Help You as a Buyer

Lenders can:

1. Reduce the interest rate. Obviously, with a reduced rate of interest, the payments will be lower and might turn a marginal buy into a good buy.
2. Lower the payments. Even if they don't change the interest rate, they can reduce the payment amount by extending the term of the loan.
3. Defer the payments. By allowing you to defer a payment or two or six, the lender can without changing the amount of the interest payment, or monthly payment, allow you some breathing room to remodel and sell a house or to fix up and find a good tenant.
4. Allow you to assume the loan without qualifying. While most loans contain language that allows a lender to accelerate (call due) a loan when a buyer purchases the property secured by the loan without the lender's permission, lenders can waive their rights to do this. They can also waive their right to call the loans for subsequent buyers.
5. Forgive late fees. A lender can waive or forgive all late fees, increased interest charges, or any other fees that may have been charged to the loan.

6. Add attorney's fees to the loan amount. Rather than requiring that you write a check for actual expenses that the lender has incurred, lenders can add them to the amount of the loan.

7. Loan you more money. If the house needs repairs, or if back taxes are unpaid, or if you need cash for another reason, you can ask the lender to increase the amount of the loan, or to make you a new second loan with terms and interest rates favorable to you.

8. Make you a loan against another property that you own. If the lender insists on a cash payment, ask to be loaned the money against another property that you own.

9. Discount an existing loan (short sale). When you acquire a property for less than the existing loan balance, you can ask the lender to accept less than what they are owed as full payment for their loan. This "short sale" will be approved by the lender only if the existing borrower does not receive any cash from the buyer.

Short Sales

For a short sale to take place, the lender will require documentation to prove that the property is being purchased for less than the loan balance. Typically, the lender will require you to furnish the following.

1. A statement from the sellers authorizing you the buyer to contact the lender on their behalf.

2. A copy of the signed contract.

3. A hardship statement from the seller explaining why the seller has not been able to make the payment or sell the property. This statement should spare no details, try to make the lender feel the pain of the seller.

4. Copies of the seller's financial statement (showing no other available resources), along with substantiation of the seller's current income (pay stubs) and expenses showing that the seller cannot afford to make the payments.

5. A copy of the closing statement (HUD 1).

6. A "net sheet"—showing all the expenses that will be deducted at closing and the net to the seller. The net to the seller should be $0.00.

7. A CMA (comparative market analysis) showing recent sales and justifying why the house is worth less than it was when it was purchased.

8. A list of any repairs needed. It is best to substantiate this list with a contractor's bid, including photos that show the damage.

9. A proof-of-funds letter.

Obviously, all this will take time and a little work. The good news is that lenders will discount a loan significantly (20%–30%) rather than face a foreclosure on a property that has dropped in value.

The bad news is that if the lender agrees to a short sale, you need to be able to write a check for the entire amount that you have agreed to pay. The lender is probably not going to make you a new loan to pay off the old loan at a discount, although this could happen if it is part of your offer. However, the lender will not allow you months to try to sell the house for more money. A short sale requires nearly immediate payment.

If you don't have the money in the bank to pay off the loan, find a line of credit for the amount you need before you make a short sale offer. As an alternative, find an investor who will fund the purchase.

Short sale deals fall apart after they are negotiated when the buyer cannot come up with the large amount of cash necessary to close the deal. Tell other investors that you have cash available for short sales and they may bring you the deals that they cannot afford.

Banks really want to get nonperforming loans off of their books. Bankers are open to all of the ideas listed above, you simply need to ask.

Dealing with Other Lenders

Although banks and other institutional lenders make the great majority of loans, each year hundreds of thousands of noninstitutional loans are originated, and you are likely to come across them as you buy. These lenders tend to be individuals or trusts and other entities for which one person is making the decisions. That gives a buyer a clear advantage, because these lenders have more motivation to solve the problem and recover their money. And, they can make a decision quickly.

Sellers Who Have Financed a Sale

In a slow market, many sellers help new buyers by lending them part or all of the purchase price. These loans are called "purchase-money mortgages," and many existing ones have nonstandard terms and paperwork. The loan documents are often prepared by an attorney or title company, and sometimes by the seller himself.

When a seller who has financed his own sale stops receiving the payments, it may cause immediate financial trauma. A seller who is used to receiving payments of $1,400 a month will notice when the money suddenly stops. The seller may be using the income to live on or to pay back another loan. Without the income, he may have an immediate and serious problem.

If a seller has financed the sale of a house in order to get rid of it, the chances are good that he won't want it back. The chances are also good that he will renegotiate the terms or even agree to a short sale as discussed above.

Family Members

Often family members loan each other money. Almost as often, those loans are not paid back. While it would ruin the conversation at a family dinner if one member was foreclosing on another, the lending relative is often very receptive to another nonrelative assuming the loan. With an intervening nonrelated investor, the lender will be more optimistic about being repaid.

If you are buying a house and one of the owner's relatives is owed part or all of the money on the loan, before you agree to buy, talk to the lending relative. This person may be happier with you making the payments. If so, you may be able to use that to your advantage and renegotiate the terms to reduce your payments or interest rate. Both of these are better solutions than a short sale, because you won't have to write a big check.

Estates

When a person dies, his or her assets become part of the estate. These assets may include loans made during the life of the deceased. They may also include property on which the estate administrator may sell and carry the financing. Eventually the estate will be distributed to the heirs. When there are more than one, it is possible that several heirs will jointly own the resulting loans. If those loans secured by real estate go into default, the estate or heirs will be very receptive to a short sale or to renegotiated terms.

As one who has served as the executor of an estate, I can tell you the executor's main interest is finishing the job. The last thing an executor or a group of heirs want would be to foreclose on a property that would require additional time to manage and sell again. Look for these situations and make them an offer to renegotiate the debt on terms that will make it profitable for you to own.

Retirement Plans

Notes, mortgages, and deeds of trust are great investments for pension plans. Like estates, they generally do not want to foreclose. They just want to keep their money invested.

A Professional Buyer's Secrets

Retirement plans possess two unique qualities. First, most plans are oriented toward the long term. Forty-year-olds with a retirement plan invested in a mortgage do not need the money for at least 20 more years. They don't really want to be paid back, but they do want to be paid. They have a lot of flexibility in how they are repaid. In my retirement plan, there are loans with no payments due for months or even years at a time. I want to keep my money invested and earning interest until I am ready to spend it, which may be 20 more years.

The second unique quality is that a retirement plan cannot deduct a loss. Since the plan pays no income taxes, a loss does it no good at all. Realizing this, you can negotiate to repay a loan that may be hard for the plan to collect.

The plan's administrators could renegotiate the terms of the loan to make it very affordable to you. Or they could agree to lend you even more money on great terms.

Case Study: Retirement Plan Loan

A retirement plan made a $150,000 loan against a house. Two years later, the borrowers stopped making payments.

The balance on the loan with six back payments was now $152,000 and the house had fallen in value to $140,000. If the retirement plan forecloses, it would have to pay attorney's fees, lose interest during the foreclosure period and marketing period (if the borrowers file for bankruptcy, the foreclosure would take longer), pay for any repairs the house may need, pay the taxes and insurance during the foreclosure period and marketing period, and then pay a commission to sell the house.

Table 15–1 shows a projected net sheet.

Table 15–1   Projected Net Sheet

Sale price in 8 months	$140,000
Less attorney's fees	$3,000
Lost interest for 8 months	$8,010
Taxes and insurance	$2,800
Fix-up cost	$5,000
Commission	$8,400
Total projected expenses	$27,210
Projected net proceeds	$112,790

Remember the motivation is twofold. One, the plan doesn't want to take a loss; and two, the plan is a long-term lender with other assets.

One offer would be to buy the house, taking over the $152,000 loan balance, and reducing the payments to $700 a month for the next 5 years, then to $800 a month for the 5 years after that, then $900 a month until repaid, all at an interest rate of 6%. You would probably pay off the loan long before the last payment became due, but more important, your payments would be low and affordable for the first 10 years. The pension plan would be able to keep the entire $152,000 loan on its books, and eventually receive every dime of their money, which would continue to accumulate interest. Compare that with the amount that the pension plan would receive in the sale outlined above.

Another offer would be to buy this house and take over the existing loan if the plan would make you a loan on another property that you own or want to buy. That loan would be at a favorable rate, say 6%, and have payments low enough to allow you to have immediate cash flow as you collected the rent. With this solution, the plan not only gets to collect its full amount on the existing loan (without the hassle of foreclosing and remarketing) and makes another solid loan, which will earn interest.

Other Individual Lenders

Other people have sold property and are holding a mortgage or deed of trust. When these loans go into default, these sellers, like most, would like to avoid the work and expense involved. Use the above case study as a guide and make them an offer that puts you in a position to have cash flow on the property that you are buying.

Unintentional Lenders–Lien Holders

Some people end up with liens against a property as a result of a lawsuit, or dissolution of a partnership, or divorce. These "lenders" are often in junior or inferior position, meaning that there are loans or liens in front of them. Because they did not intentionally make a loan, and may not be receiving payments, these lenders are very receptive to discounting their liens today for a cash payment.

Before making an offer to pay off a lien secured by a property that you are buying, learn more about the loan. How old is it? How big is it? Does the current holder of the lien have hard cash invested or was it awarded for damages in a lawsuit?

I have acquired some junior liens for as little as 5 cents on a dollar after researching the lien and determining that the holder had given up hope of collecting and would be happy with any payment. Others are well secured, but nearly all will accept a discounted amount for cash today, rather than hope to be paid later.

16

Buying Foreclosures

When a borrower cannot find a solution with a lender, the ultimate result is a foreclosure sale or trustee sale. In some states, loans against property are secured by mortgages and those states require a foreclosure process. A foreclosure is a lawsuit filed by the lender and asking a judge to issue an order to have the property sold to satisfy the debt owed. The foreclosure sale must be advertised properly to meet the legal requirement for public notice, and then the sale is open to the public.

The location and time of the sale will be advertised weeks in advance. The advertisement will be in a local paper. Find out which paper in your area runs these ads and start reading them. Notice changes in the numbers of ads. Look for addresses, names, and subdivisions that you know and go see these houses. Follow up by going to the sale and observing both how bids are made and how much the property sells for.

The location of the foreclosure sale may be the property itself, but it is most often at a courthouse or other public building. The process is designed to get the highest bid for the property so that the lender can be repaid.

In other states, loans are secured by a trust deed; a trustee, who is not a judge, handles the sale. The trustee sets the sale date and time. There is a significant difference in these processes, although both result in an auction. The entire process in a trustee state may take a month or two compared with a judicial foreclosure in other states that will often take six months to complete.

Learn more about your process by attending auctions and asking questions of the trustee or clerk conducting the sale. An experienced trustee or real estate attorney can provide a wealth of information. An additional source may be a class on real estate law taught at a local college. Hiring an attorney to represent you in a foreclosure purchase is a good investment; a mistake can cost you your entire bid.

The day of the auction, bidders will gather at the advertised location well before the sale. Remember to look for the professional bidders: they understand the process and have the resources to bid, and will often hang back until the sale begins.

Bidders are required to bring a cashier's check or cash for either a percentage of their bid or the entire bid. Some auctions allow a percentage of the bid to be paid at the conclusion of the sale with the balance due *later that day*. Others require all cash at the conclusion of the sale. There is a lot to learn about your local sales before you begin making bids.

Buying at the foreclose sale can be dangerous for several reasons.

1. The title you get is not guaranteed or insured. When you buy at a foreclosure auction, the burden is on the buyer to research the title and to know what they are bidding on. No title insurance is available and the judge or trustee will not

stand behind or warrant the title. An understanding of title law is critical, and researching the file to ensure that all required parties received proper notice of the sale is the responsibility of the buyer, not the trustee or judge.

If someone has a claim against the property and does not receive proper notice that their claim is about to be erased by a foreclosure sale, then their claim is not extinguished. It will still be a lien against the property and can be enforced by the holder. Occasionally, a junior lien will not be extinguished because improper notice is given to the holder of the lien by the filing attorney.

Sometimes a second mortgagee or trustee is foreclosing, and the first mortgage or deed of trust will still be in place after the sale. Once an unhappy buyer at a foreclosure sale contacted me after bidding on what he thought was a low amount for the purchase of a house, only to find out after the sale that it was a foreclosure by a second mortgage holder, not the first. The first

---

Case Study: Foreclosure of a Junior Lien

House value:	$200,000–$225,000
First mortgage:	$150,000
Second mortgage	$75,000
Winning bid at the foreclosure sale:	$60,000
Total price paid by winner:	
$150,000	first mortgage (not extinguished at the sale)
+ $60,000	cash bid
$210,000	

The bidder paid $210,000 for a house worth $200,000.

mortgage of more than $150,000 was still on the property and he had acquired the property subject to that mortgage. He had paid far more than the property was worth.

Only liens that are properly notified and are junior to (recorded after) the lien being foreclosed are wiped out by a foreclosure sale. All others remain on the property.

2. It's often hard to determine what condition the property will be in when you get possession. If the house is still occupied, sometimes you can offer the homeowners some cash if they leave the house empty and clean. They will need it to move. If the owners are totally uncooperative, they may leave angry. Remember: angry now-former homeowners can do a lot of damage on the way out of a house. They may take all the appliances and light fixtures and even the plumbing fixtures. Sometimes they take the cabinets and even the air-conditioner. Once after buying an empty house at foreclosure, I immediately went to secure the house and found the neighbors digging up all of the landscaping. They said that the owners gave it to them.

It's a good idea to go meet the neighbors before the sale and even to hire the neighbor to take care of the yard and watch the house for you. Most neighbors will be glad that you are buying a nuisance house and plan on improving it.

Some properties will be vacant at the time of the sale. If the house is locked up, you may not be able to check the condition of the interior or the plumbing, electrical, and mechanical systems. Contact the lender on an empty house to see if you might be able to get access. If the windows are boarded up and the locks were changed, you may be able to talk your way into the house by telling them that you want to bid on it.

If you can't get in, assume the worst and adjust your bid accordingly. Foreclosures often sell for 50 percent of retail price and one of the reasons is the uncertainty of the condition.

3. Because purchase is for all cash, the price you bid needs to be well below your estimate of the fair market price. It's not possible to get a mortgage to purchase a foreclosure, so you have to have the cash, or borrow it without using the property that you are acquiring as collateral. If you borrow from a "hard money lender" (a professional high-risk lender), you will often pay about twice the going interest rate or higher.

Your carrying costs will be high, your repair costs will be high, so bid low!

After the Sale–A Better Time to Buy a Foreclosure

If the preceding section scared you, good! A foreclosure sale is not a good place to buy your first house. In fact, many people who have invested successfully for years have never bought at a foreclosure sale. It is not the only way to make a great deal on a foreclosure.

A safer time to buy a foreclosed property is just after the sale. At a foreclosure sale either the lender who is foreclosing will end up with the property, or a bidder will bid enough that the lender will accept the bid rather than claim the property. The high bid does not have to be the full amount of the loan balance. A lender can elect to accept a lower bid.

Case Study: Foreclosure Sale for Less than Loan Balance	
House value:	$150,000–$175,000
First mortgage balance:	$154,000
High bid at the foreclosure sale:	$112,000
Total price paid by winning bidder:	$112,000

The lender accepted the $112,000 cash rather than take title to a house that needed an unknown amount of work in a changing market. If the market was strong and the house in good condition, then the lender might have decided to take the house and try to recover more money.

Buy from a Lender Who Gets Stuck with the Property

As a lender who has been stuck with a few properties, I can tell you that a lender is eager to talk to a potential buyer after the lender takes title to a foreclosure.

The challenge you have when dealing with a large institutional lender is getting to the person who will make a decision to sell the property. Large banks have a separate department that does nothing but sell the property that a bank accidentally takes title to through foreclosure. Often called the Real Estate Owned (REO) Department, the file on the foreclosed property will eventually find its way to someone's desk in that department.

Many banks immediately list the property with one broker in a town that specializes in selling REO properties. They often have crews that do repairs and maintain the property while it's on the market. If you begin watching for foreclosures in your neighborhoods, you will notice that often the same salesmen will list all of the foreclosures. Call them and let them know that you are an interested buyer.

Another strategy is to professionally approach the lender. You need to be persistent as you are dealing with a large bureaucracy. Just to get a live person on the phone can be a challenge and test your patience. If the property is one that the bank really does not want to own, typically one needing a lot of work or one in uncertain condition, they will be more anxious to do business.

Start by contacting the local branch of the lender. If it's a small bank, contact the loan officer who made the loan. If it's a large regional bank, ask them for the name and number of the REO department that handles property in your area. Then call and stay on the phone until you actually talk to a person. It's tedious work, but the reward is worth it. Our daughter once secured one of only1,500 student tickets to a national championship football game by aggressively calling (while more than 80,000 students watched from home). Your odds are better.

Bob Bruss, the writer of several excellent newspaper columns and newsletters (www.bobbruss.com), suggests sending the president of the bank a certified letter with a contract to buy the house along with a certified check for a deposit. While the president of a large bank will just refer this to the REO department, when it comes from the president's desk, it will certainly get better attention than if you just mailed it to the bank's address. Very clever.

Even the big banks have people making decisions. Work hard to locate and then build a relationship with a decision maker in the REO department. It will pay dividends.

It takes effort to buy a house directly from a lender after the foreclosure and before it is listed with a broker. If you really want the house it is worth the effort. If you are unable to get through to the lender, then wait and make your offer through the broker.

Successful buyers do what less successful buyers refuse to do!

Banks are not the only lenders foreclosing. When you notice a trustee, an individual, a corporation, a partnership, or an executor filing a foreclosure action on a house that you want to buy, go see them. Odds are good that they would much rather have money than the property.

Buying a Loan before It Is Foreclosed

While lenders cannot sell a property until after a foreclosure sale, they can sell a loan that is in foreclosure. Many of my best deals have resulted from buying a loan from a lender who did not want to foreclose. When you approach a lender before the sale, it is typical to ask for a loan balance or to make a short sale offer. Another approach is to simply offer to buy the loan, and then you can

---

Case Study: Buying a Loan before Foreclosure

This house was abandoned and damaged significantly by the owners before leaving. The banker was appropriately concerned, because he had no idea how much it would take to make the repairs. Because the house was open, I was able to do a thorough inspection (and then lock the house up) and I knew about what the repair costs would be.

House value:	$175,000–$200,000 (after $20,000 in repairs)
First mortgage balance:	$125,000
First offer to buy loan:	$80,000
Banks counteroffer:	$90,000
Final offer accepted by both:	$87,000

---

either foreclose and get title to the property, or renegotiate with the owners.

Buying from the Lender on Terms

As stated earlier, at a foreclosure sale the terms are all cash. If you wait until after the sale, you can ask the lender, whoever she or he is, to finance the property for you. A lender, large or small, would rather have a mortgage, and an income, than an empty house that has to be managed. You can often negotiate better-than-market terms when you buy from a lender. Remember, the lender is not lending you cash. She is getting rid of a problem. It's a different person making the decision than the loan office taking applications downstairs.

The bank can be flexible on the requirements for great credit and a normal down payment if it doesn't want the property. The more property a lender has in inventory, the less she wants more.

Buying Foreclosures

When a market slows quickly, lenders can accumulate inventories of thousands of empty houses. They will make nearly any kind of deal to get rid of those houses.

Here are some terms you can ask for when buying a foreclosure from a bank.

- A lower-than-market interest rate

- An interest-only loan

- A loan with less than interest-only payments (negative amortization)

- A loan with no payment for three months (first payment due in three months)

- A loan that can be assumed without qualification by another buyer

- A "no doc" loan, one that requires no qualifying

- A loan that does not require taxes and insurance to be escrowed

Buying from the Winning Bidder at the Sale

Most people who bid and buy at foreclosure auctions are not buying a house to move into; they are buying a house they hope to sell for a profit. If the house that sells at auction is one on which you made an offer, approach the winning bidder. You know how much the buyer paid for it; you just watched him buy it. He has not owned it very long so he may be willing to sell to you for a small profit.

Buying from the winning bidder is much safer than buying at the sale. Now you will have time to have the title examined and buy title insurance. Now you will have time to borrow money from a lender and negotiate a low interest rate.

One other possibility is that the high bidder may be willing to finance the sale for you. This would save you much of the cost of getting a new commercial loan.

You can agree to buy the house in "as is" condition subject to inspecting the house. If you find too much wrong with it, you can renegotiate the price or walk away from the deal.

Sharing the Profits with the Winning Bidder

If you know the bidder, or know that he is reputable, you may want to make a different type of an offer that would allow you to buy the property with a very low down payment. A seller may hold out for a larger profit than you are willing to pay today; however, you may be willing to pay a seller part of a profit that you make later.

A solution to this problem is to buy part interest in the house from the successful buyer with a note payable interest-only until the house sells. If your agreement is to share profits 50/50, then you would buy half interest in the house for half of what the buyer paid at the sale. You would then receive half the profits and the buyer would get his original investment back plus half of the profits.

Case Study: Sharing the Profits

House value:	$175,000–$200,000
Purchase at foreclosure sale:	$100,000
Purchase one-half interest:	$50,000

When property is sold, the foreclosure buyer will receive the first $100,000, plus half of the difference. Assume the house is sold for $200,000 after one year.

Sale Price:	$200,000

	Buyer	You
Half the proceeds	$100,000	$100,000
The note you owe to buyer	+$50,000	−$50,000
Cash distributed at sale	$150,000	$50,000

You might be able to buy the house for less than $150,000 right after the sale, but that would require you to borrow the money from another source and make monthly payments. Buying just half allows you to make payments only on your half of the purchase price ($50,000). If the interest rate was 8%, your interest cost for the year would be only $4,000 (8% $\times$ $50,000). If you rent the house during the year, your half of the rent should more than cover that cost.

The foreclosure buyer will make a $50,000 profit with little work (you are doing the work). This is more than he would receive with a quick "as is" sale.

Relationships between moneyed buyers (who have been investing successfully for years) and new investors (who are eager to do the work for part of the profit) are common and good for both. Get to know the buyers at your foreclosure sales and look for one that you can work with.

Getting the Owners Out after You Buy

How do you get owners to move out of their home when they lose the house in a foreclosure action? Help them. They probably need moving money and maybe a place to store much of their stuff if they are moving into a smaller place, like an apartment. Often they can rent an apartment with little up-front money, but need a storage unit.

Whenever you buy a house in a foreclosure, make sure you build enough money into the deal to help the owners move to another place. Prepay the rent on a storage unit for a year and give them enough to rent another place or move back to where their parents live. Give them enough to rent a truck if they are moving out of town. It is false economy to just try to talk them out of their house. The money you spend on helping the former owner move will be far less than you would spend evicting them and then cleaning up the mess and damage that is left behind.

17

Borrowing on Creative Terms–Your Key to Cash Flow

You can buy a particular type of property for cash flow, like a duplex, an apartment building, or a motel. I've tried them all and will tell you that managing the tenants that occupy these properties is work.

You can also get cash flow from easier-to-manage properties like houses, by borrowing on good terms when you buy. By working smart rather than working hard, you can actually have more cash flow.

Some wannabe investors borrow on bad terms and then try to squeeze more cash flow out of their tenants. Locally, an inexperienced buyer financed an investment house purchase on her credit card. Her interest rate started low, but when she missed one payment the interest rate jumped to 22%. She tried renting the house to three roommates to generate more cash flow to cover her payments. Bad plan—working hard, not smart.

If you are like me, you want the fewest tenants possible. You want to buy properties that are easiest to manage.

You can have more cash flow, not by squeezing more tenants into your properties, but by getting better terms when you borrow money.

There are many ways that you can borrow money to finance a house. Table 17–1 is a list of several kinds of loans available in my town today.

You Get to Choose the Rate of Interest You Pay

Every time you borrow money, you get to choose who to borrow from and what rate you will pay. Most investors pay retail interest rates when they borrow, and pay retail prices when they buy. By "retail" I mean the undiscounted market price. If you buy an investment house at a retail price and then pay a retail interest

Table 17–1

Source	Interest Rate
Credit card loan	6–24% (when you are late on a payment, the rate jumps)
Hard money lenders	12–18% (they lend based on the equity)
Commercial banks	8–12% (credit required—loan can be unsecured)
Banks	7–12% (rate depends on your credit)
Passive investors	8–12% (rate depends on your history)
Lenders who own property	5–12% (rate depends on your credit and skill)
Seller financing	0–12% (rate depends on your skill)

Case Study: House Bought at Retail Price and Financed at a Retail Interest Rate

House value: $215,000–$240,000
Purchase price: $215,000
Net monthly rental income: $1,200

Table 17–2 shows the amount that can be borrowed and repaid with $1,200 a month at different interest rates on a 30-year amortizing loan.

Table 17–2

Interest Rate	Term	Payment Amount
6%	30 Years	$200,150
7%	30 Years	$180,369
8%	30 Years	$163,540
9%	30 Years	$149,138
10%	30 Years	$136,740
11%	30 Years	$126,007
12%	30 Years	$116,662

If you could borrow at 6% interest, you could buy the house with about a $15,000 down payment, plus any closing costs. At a more realistic 8%, you would have to put more than $50,000 down plus your closing costs. Unless you are starting with a lot of money and great credit, this strategy is not for you. Even if you have a lot of money and great credit, you are giving up a lot of profit when you pay retail prices and interest.

rate, you would have to make a large down payment for the cash flow from the rents to cover your payments.

In his book *Nothing Down*, one of my former students, Robert Allen, explains some of the ideas I teach about buying with leverage. One of the problems he discusses concerns buying a house with nothing down, which leaves you owing a lot. Obviously, if you buy with nothing down and can't afford the payments, you will not own the property long enough to make a profit.

You have to be a clever borrower to buy with nothing down and have positive cash flow. It can be done: I've done it many times. The key is to either have the seller lend you the entire purchase price with payments that are covered by the net rent, or take over an existing loan that has low payments.

Case Study: Owner Financing with Low Payments

House value:	$215,000–$240,000
Purchase price:	$180,000
Net monthly rental income:	$1,200
Seller financing:	$180,000 @ 7%
Monthly payments:	$1,000 for first 5 years
	$1,200 for next 5 years
	$1,400 until fully paid

With this payment schedule, the payments for the first 5 years would be less than interest on the loan (which would be $1,050). The balance at the end of 5 years would be $183,580. When the payments increase to $1,200, it will begin amortizing, and as they increase again, the loan will pay off completely in about 28 years.

Many sellers want a long-term income stream. One seller, who we paid off early, was upset: he knew that when he took our money and put it in the bank, his monthly income would drop dramatically.

Keeping the payments low for the first 5 to 10 years is most important for you. In 10 years, both the rents and property value will increase. You should be able to refinance and pay off your seller, and the higher rents will be enough to pay off your new loan.

Another Way to Buy with Nothing Down and Have Cash Flow

Earlier I explained how to take over an existing loan. Here is an example showing the advantage of assuming or taking subject to an existing loan on the property. Again, this is a nothing-down purchase with terms that will produce immediate cash flow for the buyer.

Case Study: Taking Over a Loan with Low Payments

House value:	$250,000–$300,000
Purchase price:	$225,000
Net monthly rental income:	$1,300
Existing bank financing:	$178,000 (@ 6.5%, 30 years)
Monthly payments:	$1,125
Balance due to seller:	$47,000 (4% interest)
Payment on note to seller:	$100 per month for first five years
	$200 per month for next five years
	$300 per month until paid

This loan has less than interest-only payments for the first five years, then it amortizes. Often, sellers of a house like this will call and ask for their money soon, and will offer to take a discounted amount if you pay them early. This can increase your profits by tens of thousands of dollars.

Both of these ways just described to buy and finance houses work well in a changing market where sellers are unable to sell quickly. One feature of the two seminars I teach each year has students actually finding motivated sellers of houses and making them offers. More than 100 houses have been purchased during my classes over the years.

What Are Good Terms Worth to You?

When you borrow on better-than-market terms, how much additional profit are you making? If a seller will lend money at 6% and it costs 8% to borrow from the bank, how much is that loan worth to you each month as a buyer?

Table 17–3 shows how much monthly profit can be earned by borrowing from sellers instead of a bank.

Table 17–4 shows how much more you would make over the term of a 30-year loan.

Although it takes more work to buy a house with owner financing, it pays well.

When I started buying property, the only way I could buy was with terms like the ones outlined in the preceding two case studies on pages 176 and 177. It takes more work to find sellers who will finance property for you, but if you have little cash or credit, it will always be a way that you can buy property.

Table 17–3 Additional Monthly Profit Earned by Borrowing from Sellers

Bank Interest Rate	Seller Interest Rate	Loan Amount	Additional Monthly Profit Earned
8%	6%	$100,000	$167
8%	6%	$150,000	$250
8%	6%	$200,000	$333
8%	6%	$250,000	$416
8%	6%	$300,000	$500

Table 17–4   Profit Earned over a 30-Year Period by Borrowing from Sellers

Bank Interest Rate	Seller Interest Rate	Loan Amount	Additional 30-Year Profit
8%	6%	$100,000	$60,120
8%	6%	$150,000	$90,000
8%	6%	$200,000	$119,880
8%	6%	$250,000	$149,760
8%	6%	$300,000	$180,000

Using Investor Money to Fund Your Deals

Many people with money like and understand real estate, but they do not have the time or ambition to buy and manage property. They probably have their money invested in the stock market or in a bank account. There are two major differences between investing in the stock market and investing in real estate. First, you can use knowledge and skills to buy a property at a below-market price and on better-than-market terms. Second, you can buy real estate with little or nothing down.

A stockbroker will tell you that real estate is not liquid. That's the best part. Because it is not liquid and is harder to sell, you can make a significant "going in" profit. In the stock market, you pay the same price as everyone else, regardless of how good you are.

Another good thing about real estate being illiquid is that it is easier to hold it until it at least doubles in value. How many people hold a stock until it doubles in value? Not many will, because—at least in part—it is so easy to sell a stock. Most stockholders who have a 50% or 75% profit get nervous and sell before it goes back down.

Because real estate tends to have a one-track mind when it comes to which way to go, it pays to hold it, even when the market is not moving much. In the long run it will move up. Many investors desire this result, but because it takes extra effort, few investors actually achieve it.

Once you acquire the skills to buy a property below the market and manage it well, you can attract investors who can: (1) be a source of down payment money, (2) be a source of credit for acquiring loans, and (3) be a source of loans for property that you want to own by yourself. When two people invest together, profits can be shared in many ways. Simply borrowing money from an investor at an agreed-upon interest rate is the simplest and best for you—as long as you can afford to make the payments.

Case Study: Borrowing from an Investor

House value:	$250,000–$300,000
Purchase price:	$200,000
Net monthly rental income:	$1,350
Loan from investor:	$200,000 @ (8% interest only due in 10 years or upon sale)
Monthly payments:	$1,333

This loan would be secured by a first mortgage or deed of trust on the property. An interest-only loan has several advantages. First, the bookkeeping is easy. The balance will always be $200,000 (plus any interest owed). Second, it will have lower payments, which is good for you as the borrower. Third, the investor's full $200,000 stays invested at 8%. If, for example, you start repaying him $75 a month from the principal, it would probably go into a bank account earning far less than 8%.

With this arrangement, you are taking all of the risk, but will benefit from all of the profit from the sale. Because you bought it $50,000 below the market, and with nothing down, you will be well rewarded for your risk.

The lender is lending only 80% of the property's value ($200,000/$250,000 = 0.80) If the lender wants more commitment on your part, you could make a down payment, which would then reduce your monthly payments. Another alternative is to give the lender additional collateral. The collateral could be a bank account that you pledge, or a bond or any securities. It could also be another property that you own.

Lenders with $200,000 are more concerned about taking a risk with their money than earning a high return. They will want a higher return than they can get at a bank, but they are primarily concerned with safety. If you own another property and are willing to pledge it as additional collateral for the loan, you might be able to negotiate a lower interest rate.

Whenever you pledge additional collateral, build in a provision in the mortgage or deed of trust that allows you to release that collateral with the payment of a certain amount. If your lender gives you a choice of making a $25,000 down payment or pledging additional collateral, then it is logical that if you pay her the $25,000 the collateral will be released from the loan. This allows you to sell the property pledged as additional collateral by paying down only $25,000 of the remaining loan balance.

Case Study: Buying with an Investor

House value:	$300,000–$350,000
Purchase price:	$250,000
Down payment:	$50,000
Net monthly rental income:	$1,400
Existing bank financing:	$200,000 (@ 6.5%, 30 years)
Monthly payments:	$1,264

While you may not have had $50,000 in the bank, or may be unwilling to put $50,000 down on this house, it is an excellent deal to share with an investor.

Assume that after you buy together, you hold the house until it doubles in value:

House value at resale:	$600,000
Remaining loan balance:	$180,000 (approximation)
Gross profit:	$420,000
Less the initial investment:	$50,000
Profit to be split:	$370,000
50%:	$185,000

The investor would make a $185,000 before-tax profit on his initial $50,000 investment. In addition he would have received one-half of the cash flow during the holding period. You would also receive $185,000 for your share, plus half of the cash flow. Most investors would be happy with this return, especially if you do all of the work.

Here are a few suggestions for investing with others.

1. Only buy properties that produce a profit immediately. The reason to use an investor's cash is to do two things.
   a. Drive the price down to a wholesale price
   b. Reduce the amount of debt necessary to buy the property
2. Only buy with one other investor at a time.
3. Have a written agreement on how you will split profits and who will be responsible for and have the authority to make decisions about selling and renting.
4. Have a mutual understanding about how long you will hold the property. It's better to state this in terms of profit instead of time. For example, you could agree to hold the property until its value doubles (or it reaches a certain value). If this

takes 5 years or 10 years, you have a target. You can always modify this by mutual consent.

5. Only buy properties with someone who has the money in the bank (or in a securities account), not someone who has to borrow it to give it to you. If they have to borrow it, they will be anxious to repay it and will want to sell sooner.

Do not buy a house with an investor until you develop the skills necessary to buy and manage property.

18

Selling in a Market with Few Buyers

In a buyer's market, the buyers rule. They have the upper hand because there are more properties on the market than buyers. Some of those properties sit on the market for months or years. This is a great time to buy, as you can target a seller who you think needs to sell and then make an offer that guarantees you a profit.

It's a challenging time to sell—but you can sell with the right strategy. Even in a very slow market, there are always potential buyers—you just have to give them a reason to buy.

If you don't have to sell in a buyer's market, *don't*. Rent instead. Rental markets often improve in a buyer's market. The reason it is a buyer's market is that something has happened in the marketplace to make buying less attractive. It may be a run-up in prices. It could also be a dramatic increase in interest rates. Either of these would make it difficult for many buyers to qualify for a loan, so they become renters instead of buyers.

Many still want to buy after prices or interest rates increase, but they don't think that they can afford to buy. You can still sell a property if you show a willing buyer how she or he can afford to buy your house.

When markets slow down, sales may drop 20%, 30%, or even 50%. That still leaves another 50% that are buyers and all you need is one buyer.

Some Houses Sell Faster Than Others

One secret to selling in a slow market is buying a house to sell that has wide appeal. Houses in certain price ranges sell faster as there are more buyers in that price range. You can find out which price ranges sell fastest from a Realtor or other real estate agent who has access to MLS (Multiple Listing Service) statistics. Look at the "time on the market" for different price ranges. You may be able to search by neighborhoods.

Houses in more desirable neighborhoods sell faster than the average house. Look for a neighborhood with houses in the price range that you want to buy in that has a shorter-than-average sales times.

Another secret to selling in a slow market is to buy houses in the low end of the price range in a neighborhood.

Buy a house for under $300,000 in a neighborhood with houses ranging from $290,000 to $425,000, and it will sell faster than the houses priced over $400,000. There are simply more people who can afford the cheaper house. Often the less expensive houses have potential. They can be upgraded or expanded. The more expensive houses may already be overimproved or overbuilt for the neighborhood.

Avoid Buying "Unique" Houses

A "unique" house is hard to sell in any market, especially in a slow market. Avoid buying houses with strange exterior design and unusual floor plans. Look for normal-looking houses on average-sized and -shaped lots. Avoid corner lots or other odd-shaped lots. Avoid pools: only a fraction of buyers want a pool. Look for houses with garages and/or basements; everyone likes extra room for stuff. Garages and basements are "cheap" space, which add more than their cost to the value of a house.

Another Secret: Understanding Buyer's Motivations

Asking a few friendly questions will help you qualify potential buyers. A couple who are staying in a motel until they find a house are better candidates than another couple who have to sell the house they currently own before they can buy yours. Just as you learned to rank the seller's motivation, you can rank a potential buyer's motivation.

Ask gently probing questions like "How soon do you need to move?" and "Have you qualified for a new loan?"

Learn if they are first-time buyers, or if they owned a house before and are moving up or moving down. If they have to sell a home they own before they buy yours, they are not good prospects—spend little time with them.

Your best prospect is either (1) a buyer who has sold her home and needs to move, (2) one who is moving to town who is eager to buy, or (3) a renter who is ready to buy.

You've Got to Give Them a Reason to Buy

Many people living in an apartment or duplex with their family would rather have a house and a yard. Owning a house is the American dream.

Target renters in your town by sending them ads or postcards. Try to spark their interest with lead lines like the following.

- "Why rent when owning can be as cheap and you get to paint any color you like?"

- "Tired of walking a block to your car—buy today and park at your front door."
- "Stop flushing your rent down the toilet—start building equity next month!"

These statements capture some of the reasons that most renters would rather buy. Most who rent would like to buy, if you can show them how.

Why do renters continue to rent? Here are the top reasons.

1. Lack of a down payment and closing costs
2. Lack of income
3. Problems in qualifying for a loan

Other buyers may want your house but have other problems.

1. They have not sold their old house.
2. They are new in town and new on the job.
3. They don't have enough for a down payment and closing costs.

Another problem is a poor credit history. Be cautious of selling to someone with a poor credit record unless you are convinced that the cause was probably a one-time event, like a serious illness or a business failure. A debtor who runs up credit card debt and then refuses to pay it is a poor credit risk.

However, those buyers who have had a bankruptcy or foreclosure, might be a better risk than someone with a lot of current debt. They probably have few creditors now, and if they have turned a corner in their lives, they may be a good risk.

To sell renters a house, you will have to overcome the reasons why renters believe they can't buy. Those reasons may include (1) little money for a down payment and (2) not enough income to make a mortgage payment at this time.

If you can show them how to buy with the down payment they have and with monthly payments that they can afford, then the price you are charging for the house becomes a nonissue. You can sell a house for a retail price, even in a slow market, if you help buyers by offering terms that they can afford.

To Sell with or without a Real Estate Agent?

Selling a house is a skill. If you don't know how to do it, either learn or pay an agent to list and negotiate a sale for you. Some sellers try to sell a house by themselves for months, and then list with an agent. This is a waste of money. Either acquire the skills to sell a house yourself, or use a skilled agent to do the job for you.

If you use an agent, use one who has actually sold several houses in your neighborhood. Many agents list properties and hope other agents will sell them. You want an agent who knows how to sell and close, and who deals in your price range and area. Don't make the mistake of listing with a social acquaintance or a relative unless you are sure that they can produce results.

Using a Real Estate Agent

Real estate agents are by nature optimistic. This is not a bad thing, but it can distort reality. Reality can be expensive. For more than 10 years, I was an active Realtor and owned an office with more than a dozen associates. Real estate agents provide a valuable service for owners who don't know how to or don't want to sell their own property, but this service comes at a cost.

If you are selling a rental house using an agent, you would want to move your tenants out and fix up the house. A rented house never looks great. More important, the tenants have an interest in the house not selling, because then they will have to move. They will often make it hard to show the house.

When selling a rental house, fixing up the house and listing it requires you to give up the income the house produces and to invest additional money.

In addition to paying a real estate commission, it is likely that the offer you finally accept will be for less than the listing price.

Suppose that you list a $300,000 property with an agent, and 90 days after you list it, you accept an offer for $290,000 and pay a 6% commission of $17,400. You will net about $272,600. In addition, it will cost you at least $1,500 a month or another $4,500 in carrying costs, not accounting for repairs that you make before you market the house, or are required to make before closing. You could easily spend another $5,000 in fix-up costs or negotiated repairs.

Projected Net from Sale of Listed Property

List price:	$300,000
Offer accepted:	$290,000
Less commission:	$17,400
Less carrying costs:	$4,500
Less negotiated repairs:	$5,000
Probable net proceeds:	$263,100

Selling Your Own Property

If you learn to sell your own houses, then not only can you save a commission and some costs, you can often sell faster because you can offer better terms. A typical commission on a $300,000 house would be 6% or $18,000. I often sell houses and finance them for first-time buyers, taking as little as $5,000 for a down payment.

Selling a House to Buyers Who Need Help

Knowing how to sell your own property is a valuable skill. It is worth tens of thousands of dollars every time you sell a property. Financing a sale for a buyer, taking only a small down payment, sounds like a risky proposition. It can be unless you qualify your prospective buyers like a landlord does.

Landlords are used to letting someone move into their house after paying only one or two months' rent and a security deposit. If the rent and security deposit on a house totals $3,500, then letting someone move in with a $5,000 down payment is less risky than renting them the property.

By offering the house with a low down payment, you broaden your market and can sell faster. Although a real estate agent could offer a house on terms, he would typically want a large-enough down payment to cover his commission. If he would agree to take the commission over time as you receive your money, then an agent could help you sell.

Selling with a Low Down Payment Using a Lease Option

Using a lease option to sell allows you to sell either to an existing tenant or to another buyer who may need time to acquire a bank loan. I sell nearly all of my houses using lease options, for several reasons.

1. They sell faster. Typically it takes only a month or two to find a buyer when you offer to sell using a lease option with a low down payment and monthly payments equal to the market rent.
2. My costs are lower. The house sells faster so there are fewer vacant days; fewer bills from advertising and maintaining the house; plus, here is a big item, you can sell the house in "as is" condition. If the house has any needed repairs, disclose them, but let the buyer make the repairs. When the buyer invests her time and money improving the house, she is more likely to close. Finally, there is no commission to pay.
3. It helps first-time homebuyers to get into the housing market. Younger buyers often need help with buying their first home. Selling a young family a home on terms that they can afford not only can be profitable, but it is helpful.

Bob Bruss, a successful California house investor, recommends that when you advertise a house for sale with a lease option, you can attract buyers by stating in your ad,"$5,000 moves you in." This helps buyers self-qualify. Most buyers might think that closing costs and other expenses would add up to a higher total, so stating an inclusive number like $5,000 helps your phone ring.

Occasionally someone will respond to your ad who has more to put down, and, of course, collecting more money up-front is better for you as the seller.

When you sell on a lease option, you want the buyer to eventually be able to qualify for and obtain a conventional loan and pay you off. Often a year's term on a lease option is long enough for the buyer to qualify for a bank loan.

To improve the chances of lease option buyers closing when they purchase a house from you, you can "prequalify" your buyers, like a lender will when they apply for a loan. Conventional lenders look at borrowers' income and debts to see if they can afford a new loan. Lenders want to see no more than 28% of borrowers' gross income used for loan payments, and no more than 38% used for total debt payments.

A borrower with $3,500 a month gross income could afford monthly house payments of $980 a month (28% $\times$ $3,500 = $980) and total debt payments of $1,330 per month (38% $\times$ $3,500 = $1,330). If your buyers have higher-than-acceptable debt, they need to increase their income or reduce their debt before applying for a loan.

Selling on Terms

An alternative to using a lease option sale is to offer to finance the property for a seller. There are several differences in the two approaches.

When you agree to sell with a lease option, you have not transferred the title to the property. You still own it, and if the tenants/buyers fail to make the payments, often they will leave without any legal action having to be taken. If legal action is necessary, normally an eviction procedure is what is required to get possession of the property. Their option to buy will not be valid or enforceable unless they pay the rent.

When you sell on terms, you transfer title to the property, holding a note and mortgage (or deed of trust) as collateral. This transfer may require that local or state taxes be paid on the transfer, plus you, as the seller, may have an income tax liability.

Selling at High Prices with the Lowest Costs

You have options when you decide to sell a house. One is to sell to another investor. The advantage is that you can sell to an investor a house that is rented so you won't lose the income while the house is on the market. The disadvantage is that most investors want a good deal and would rather have you finance the property for them than borrow from a bank.

If you don't need a cash sale and collecting income from a loan fits into your overall plan, selling on terms may be a good solution.

Case Study: Selling to Another Investor or Friend or Relative

House value: $325,000–$350,000
Sale price: $349,000
Down payment: $10,000
Monthly payments: $1,695 (6% interest only)
Compare with net rental income of $1,400.

You can sell for a higher price by offering great terms, like a 6% interest-only loan for a term of 3 to 5 years. If at the end of the term, you want to continue collecting interest, you could extend the term of the loan. When you sell on terms, you can treat it as an "installment sale" for tax purposes. This allows you to pay taxes as you receive your profits. Check with your CPA to see if you qualify.

This is a good solution if you have a family member or a friend that you want to help to invest.

Selling a House That Needs Work

The condition of the house is not as critical when you are selling starter houses. Although a house in good shape will typically appeal to more buyers and sell faster, a house needing work is attractive to other buyers.

When you have a house that needs a lot of work, consider selling it in "as is" condition, but only sell to someone qualified to do the work. You don't want to get a house back in worse condition.

Case Study: Selling a House That Needs Work Using a Lease Option

House value: $250,000–$275,000
Option price: $269,000
Down payment: $5,000
Monthly rent: 1-year term: $995

Note that both the down payment and monthly payments are low for a house in this price range. This is to entice buyers and make it affordable for them during the time they are making the needed repairs to the house. Most buyers will improve the house, and then refinance it quickly to recover their investment in the house. It will be appraised at a higher price after it is repaired.

Although the great majority of the houses I sell on lease options actually close, in the event a tenant/buyer cannot close, I either offer to continue to rent the house to her (without the option) or offer to refund part of her option money if she gives me the house back on time and in good condition. Sometimes they buy another house from me later, or become a great long-term tenant.

For more information on lease options, see "Buying and Selling Using Lease Options," available on my Web site, www.johnschaub.com.

Because of several instances of fraudulent transactions, some states (Texas most recently) have enacted legislation that places certain requirements on lease option sales. Research your state laws before buying or selling using a lease option.

Buy/Sell Decision-Making Process for a House Bought at the Top of the Market

If you bought a house near the top of a hot market and now find that you cannot sell it for what you paid for it, you have a tough decision to make. Should you hold it empty until it sells, or should you rent it and wait for better market conditions?

Case Study: House Bought at the Top of the Market

Market price at top of market:	$300,000
Purchase price:	$280,000
Market value 6 months later:	$250,000
Monthly cost to carry house (after collecting rent):	$500
Monthly cost to carry the house for 3 years:	$18,000
Monthly cost to carry house for 5 years:	$30,000
Before-tax loss if sold today:	$30,000 ($280,000–$250,000)
Reasonable sale price to expect if held 5 years:	$325,000
Less cost of holding:	$30,000
Net profit:	$15,000

This example does not account for some increase in cash flow as you might be able to raise rents, nor does it account for any tax savings that you may realize.

The deciding factor would be the location of the house and the type of financing you have. If the financing and location are both better than average, then holding the house is a wise decision. If the house will be a management problem because of a bad location or poor construction, or if the loan is not a below-market loan which gives you leverage that improves your profits over time, then selling today would be advisable.

Although selling in a flat market or a declining market is more challenging than in a hot market, sales happen.

19

A 10-Year Plan for Building Wealth One House at a Time

My dad came to me when he was in his sixties and asked me to help him begin investing for retirement. Up to that point, his strategy had been to carry enough life insurance to pay off his debts when he died. I suspect that he was as surprised as anyone that he was still alive at 63, because he had always lived life to its fullest.

Once he celebrated his sixty-third birthday, he concluded that he might live even longer. To enjoy life he would need more money than he had saved to date. I helped him buy several houses, and today at age 90, he has several thousand dollars a month of extra cash flow from his three free-and-clear houses. Those extra funds allow him to live very comfortably.

It's Never Too Late to Start

You don't know how long you are going to live. Some medical scientists believe that we may outlive our parents by 20 years or more. By actively investing, you can stay sharp and stay in control of your finances. Plus, it's a lot more fun to talk about a deal you just made than your aches and pains.

Putting Together Your 10-Year Plan

Ten years is long enough to acquire a significant amount of wealth by investing in houses. Table 19–1 is an example of a 10-year house investment plan.

The plan assumes that the house you would buy in your town is worth $250,000 today and that it will double in value in 10 years. It also assumes that you learn to buy that house at least 10% under the market and then finance with a 10% down payment with terms that will allow you to hold it until it doubles in value. If houses take longer than 10 years to double in your town, then your market may be a buyer's market and you should be able to make better deals when you buy. If your market is less expensive and you can still buy a house in your town for $125,000, just cut the numbers in half. The good news is that it costs less to live in your town.

If your houses are more expensive, double or triple the numbers until they match the numbers in your town. You will need more money, but the more expensive houses can be bought at a larger discount, so you will have more money. If you live in a very expensive market, then buy only one house every two or three years. You will still have enough in 10 years.

Once you own a portfolio of houses, you may decide to hold them indefinitely. If they appreciate 5% the next year, this portfolio of ten $500,000 houses would produce a profit of $250,000, not counting the rental income. If you hold them until the debt is paid off, you would have a significant income from just the rents, and could sell one for additional income if you needed to.

More Than Money

Buying a house to rent to a family who needs a decent place to live not only will make you a lot of money, but it also provides a family

Table 19–1   Your Net Worth in 10 Years If You Buy and Hold One $250,000 House a Year

Year	House Price in 10 years	Purchase Price	Approximate Loan Balance in 10 Years	Your Equity in 10 Years
1	$500,000	$225,000	$200,000	$300,000
2	$500,000	$240,000	$212,000	$288,000
3	$500,000	$255,000	$224,000	$276,000
4	$500,000	$270,000	$238,000	$262,000
5	$500,000	$290,000	$256,000	$244,000
6	$500,000	$313,000	$273,000	$227,000
7	$500,000	$338,000	$296,000	$204,000
8	$500,000	$368,000	$324,000	$176,000
9	$500,000	$404,000	$351,000	$149,000
10	$500,000	$450,000	$404,000	$96,000
Totals	$5,000,000	$3,153,000	$2,778,000	$2,222,000

with a home. Many of my tenants live in the same home 10 years or more; some tenants stayed longer than 20 years. While they may not be able to afford to own that house, they can enjoy living much of their life in a nice home in a good neighborhood.

If more investors would buy one other home as an investment, there would be plenty of affordable housing in every town. On a parallel subject, President Jimmy Carter has said that if every church in America would build just one Habitat for Humanity home, we could eliminate poverty housing in our country. Some churches have built more than 100 and are still going strong. We are making progress.

Planting Trees

The best time to plant a tree was 10 years ago. The second best time to plant one is today.

Building Real Estate Wealth in a Changing Market

Although you cannot buy houses 10 years ago, you can start today. A changing market brings opportunity. Start today to identify neighborhoods in your town that will be strong 10 years from now. Look for houses that are owned by sellers who need to sell. Make offers at least 10 percent below the market. Finance the houses with terms that you can afford for at least 10 years. Rent them at fair rents to tenants who value the house. Hold the houses until they double in value. Now enjoy the rest of your life!

"It's never too late to be what you might have been."

—George Elliot

20

Challenge Yourself: Do Something for Others

Once you find your way financially, you may ask yourself, why make more? Some compare it to climbing mountains. You climb mountains because you can; you make money because you can.

While making and spending money is fun, if that's all that you ever do, you will miss a lot of pleasure in life. The pleasure of spending time with family and friends. The pleasure of coaching children and helping them learn the value of team play or winning fairly. The pleasure of reading to a young student or giving them a scholarship so that they can be the first in their family to attend college. The pleasure of helping Habitat for Humanity homeowners build their own house, and then of watching their kids grow up in a decent home. The pleasure of listening to your father or mother or a friend tell you stories you may have heard many times, but that are always told like it's the first time.

Once you learn how to make money, then invest some time in others. Enjoy all of life's pleasures.

Contact Information

Robert Bruss, www.bobbruss.com, 251 Park Road, Burlingame,
  CA 94010
Fixer Jay DeCima, www.fixerjay.com, P.O. Box 491779, Redding,
  CA 96049
Jack Miller, www.cashflowconcepts.com, P.O. Box 21172, Tampa
  FL 33622
Peter Fortunato: www.peterfortunato.com, P.O. Box 8804,
  Madeira Beach, FL 33738

The Fuller Center for Housing
Millard and Linda Fuller
701 South Martin Luther King Boulevard
Americus, GA 31719
www.Fullercenter.org

Building Real Estate Wealth in a Changing Market

Habitat for Humanity
121 Habitat Street
Americus, GA 31709
www.habitat.org

Index

Index

Index

Index

Index

Index

Index

Index

About the Author

John Schaub is a full-time investor who has survived seven presidents, several recessions, and hundreds of tenants. John buys quality properties at discounted prices with better-than-market financing and rents them to long-term tenants.

He shares what he has learned, both good and bad, with readers and with students at three seminars a year. He buys, sells, and manages all of his properties, and continues to do what he teaches.

Profits from investing in houses have enabled John and his family to enjoy traveling the world and the freedom to take many extended vacations. John, an instrument-rated pilot, often flies his plane for business and pleasure.

John is a long-time advocate for affordable housing and has served for 21 years on the Board of Habitat for Humanity Sarasota, Inc., and 7 years on the Board of Habitat for Humanity International. He serves on the boards of The Fuller Center for Housing.

For more information about John's home
study courses and live seminars
please contact us at:

www.johnschaub.com

Special Offer–Free Bonus

Is It a Money Maker or a Money Pit?

John Schaub's Profit Matrix

Identifying and recognizing a good deal is a challenge. Professional buyers consistently buy at below market prices because they instinctively know a good deal when they see one.

John designed a decision-making matrix that you can use to quickly evaluate the potential of both the property and the seller. Use this matrix and you can avoid buying a *money pit* that will waste your time and soak up your cash, and you will know when to make your offer to get the best deal.

John has 35 years experience evaluating properties and negotiating with sellers. It all comes together in this matrix to help you make critical decisions early in the buying process.

Plus—John explains how to use his matrix in a 20-minute audio accessible on any computer online.

Simply go to John's Web page:

www.johnschaub.com

and click on the special free-offer button.